DATE DUE

MAY 2 7 2003	
JUN 2 4 2005	

DEMCO, INC. 38-2931

CULTURES OF THE WORLD®

AUSTRIA

Sean Sheehan

BENCHMARK BOOKS

MARSHALL CAVENDISH
NEW YORK

PICTURE CREDITS

Cover photo: © Christian Heeb

AFP: 30, 31, 32 • ANA Press Agency: 13, 61, 87 • Austrian Tourism Board: 1, 3, 7, 16, 38, 41, 77, 111, 113, 117, 119, 130 • Oliver Bolch: 5, 6, 17, 34, 36, 42, 43, 44, 46, 47, 49, 65, 78, 102, 106, 114, 122, 127 • Corbis: 9 • Getty Images/Hulton Archive: 62, 95 (both), 96 • Dave G. Houser/Houserstock: 26 • Image Bank: 8, 24, 29, 35, 56, 70 • Andre Laubier: 14, 21, 22, 63, 101, 103, 104 (top), 126 • Les Voyageurs: 18, 27, 80, 93, 104 (bottom), 105 • Life File Photographic Library: 11, 12, 15, 19, 20, 23, 39, 40, 51, 53, 54, 57, 58, 66, 68, 72, 74, 75, 76, 82, 83, 85, 86, 88, 94, 100, 107, 108, 109, 110, 115, 116, 118, 121, 128 • Lonely Planet Images: 45, 64, 124, 125 • K. F. Seetoh: 4, 52, 60, 67, 69, 71, 73, 79, 91, 92, 97, 98, 99, 123 • David Simson: 48, 50, 84, 89 • Topham Picturepoint: 131

PRECEDING PAGE

Austrians in a village celebrate when farmers come down the mountains with their herds.

Marshall Cavendish Corporation
99 White Plains Road
Tarrytown, NY 10591
Website: www.marshallcavendish.com

© 1992, 2003 by Times Media Private Limited
All rights reserved. First edition 1992. Second edition 2003.

Originated and designed by
Times Books International, an imprint of
Times Media Private Limited, a member of
Times International Publishing

Printed in Singapore

Library of Congress Cataloging-in-Publication Data
Sheehan, Sean, 1951–
　　Austria / by Sean Sheehan.—2nd ed.
　　　　p. cm.—(Cultures of the world)
　　Summary: Presents the geography, history, economy, and social life and customs of Austria, the birthplace of such people as Kurt Waldheim, Wolfgang Amadeus Mozart, Sigmund Freud, and Arnold Schwarzenegger.
　　Includes bibliographical references and index.
　　ISBN 0-7614-1497-5
　　1. Austria—Juvenile literature. 2. Austria—History—Juvenile literature—Juvenile literature. 3. Austria—Social life and customs—Juvenile literature. [1. Austria.] I. Title. II. Cultures of the world (2nd ed.)
DB17.S44 2002
943.6—dc21　　　　　　　　　　　　　2002011623

7 6 5 4 3

CONTENTS

Skiing down snowy slopes in Austria in the wintertime.

Riding sleds down grassy slopes in Austria in the summertime.

INTRODUCTION

THE REPUBLIC OF AUSTRIA is one of the smaller countries in the European Union (EU), occupying 32,367 square miles (83,830 square km) in south-central Europe. The dramatic, snowcapped mountains of the Austrian Alps, part of a range characterized by jagged peaks and raging rivers, attract skiers from all over the continent.

Monasteries and convents from as early as the eighth century dot the landscape of this modern republic, home to eight World Heritage sites. Castles and palaces attest to Austria's imperial past, when it governed a vast and powerful empire.

Austria is the birthplace of some of the world's most beautiful music. The Bonn-born Beethoven settled in Vienna because it was the music capital of the world. Salzburg, where Mozart was born, holds music events throughout the year.

GEOGRAPHY

AUSTRIA IS A LANDLOCKED COUNTRY in south-central Europe. It is bordered by Germany, the Czech Republic, and Slovakia to the north, Hungary to the east, Slovenia and Italy to the south, and Switzerland and Liechtenstein to the west. Austria stretches 362 miles (583 km) from east to west and 162 miles (261 km) from north to south.

Austria's main geographical feature is the Alpine mountain system crossing the country from east to west. The Alps dominate the southern and central parts of the country. Only in the north does the land flatten out into a plateau drained by the Danube River that flows eastward.

Below: **Mieminger Plateau in Tirol, a classic Austrian scene with mountains, trees, pastures, and even a castle.**

Opposite: **Alpine flowers and a view of Wildspitze, Austria's second highest mountain at 12,382 feet (3,774 m).**

7

Austria's fertile valleys are ideal for agriculture.

THE AUSTRIAN ALPS

The most dramatic feature of Austria's landscape, the Alps cover 64 percent of the country—from the Swiss border in the west, across the central region, and almost to the Vienna Basin in the east.

The Alps were formed some 30 million years ago when tremendous disturbances deep in the earth created pressures so strong that they caused large areas of rock to fold and rise high above the ground. At altitudes of more than 6,000 feet (1,828 m), snow is present at least half the year. On the higher peaks, the snow never melts. In the foothills and valleys of the mountains, rich pasture lands and alluvial soils have enabled farmers to make Austria almost self-sufficient in food production.

The northern Alps extend from Vorarlberg province in the west, east through central Salzburg, and to the Vienna Woods. They are the most inaccessible part of the Alps. The southern limestone Alps, which run along Austria's border with Italy and Slovenia, include the Karawanken range south of the Drava River in the province of Carinthia. In the central Alps, which contain the country's highest and most famous mountain, the Grossglockner, granite, gneiss, and schist have weathered over millions of years to form spectacular features.

CROSSING THE ALPS

Two important gaps in the mountains link Austria to neighboring countries—the Arlberg Pass in the west leading to Switzerland and the Brenner Pass going south to Italy. When it snows heavily, the Arlberg Pass may have to be closed, but traffic from Switzerland can continue moving into the Voralberg area through a tunnel under the pass. Ski resorts flourish in the Arlberg area due to the long winters.

The Brenner Pass is especially important for its low-lying position. Winter snows never block the pass, so it remains open throughout the year. The pass has been a major route for traffic moving from Italy to Germany for centuries. Today, roads and train lines continue to link the two countries.

AN ALPINE CITY

The mostly flat city of Innsbruck is nestled some 2,000 feet (600 m) above sea level on the margins of the central Alps in the valley of the green Inn River.

A 10,827-foot (3,300-m) cable-car ride starting from either the Hafelekar terminal at 7,444 feet (2,269 m) or Seegrube at 6,250 feet (1,905 m) offers a bird's eye view of the Nordkette peaks, which form a spectacular backdrop to this Alpine city. Innsbruck's landscape provides great opportunities for skiing, hiking, and cycling.

Trains leaving from Innsbruck's main station, the Hauptbahnhof, pass plateau villages such as Reith and Seefeld.

The city of Innsbruck in the central Alps.

9

GLACIERS

Glaciers are large masses of moving ice formed in conditions typically found in high mountain regions like the Austrian Alps. Snow collects in the folds of the mountains, and as more snow piles on, the lower layers turn into ice under the weight of the upper layers. When the ice is about 200 feet (60 m) thick, it begins to slowly slide down the valley floor. Glaciers in the highest summits, where the temperatures at the base of the ice masses are lowest, may move as little as 3.3 feet (1 m) a year.

A glacier is like a gigantic earthmover, scraping and grooving the bedrock of the valley and making the original fold in the mountains larger and deeper. The result, a U-shaped glacial valley, is a typical feature of the Austrian landscape. Most of the country's villages and small towns are tucked into these valleys.

At the head of a glacier valley, moving ice erodes the rock and carves a deep bowl-like basin called a cirque. Sometimes two cirques form side by side so that all that remains of the original mountain between them is a narrow ridge called an arête. This accounts for the slender but high mountains found in the Austrian Alps. Parallel cirques may meet at some point, crossing the arête and forming a pass called a col.

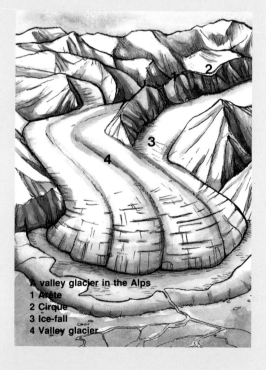

A valley glacier in the Alps
1 Arête
2 Cirque
3 Ice-fall
4 Valley glacier

A valley after the effects of glaciation
1 A U-shaped valley
2 Hanging valley
3 Waterfall

A winter scene at Bad Hofgastein.

CLIMATE

Winter temperatures in Austria range from 34 to 39°F (1 to 4°C), summer temperatures from 68 to 77°F (20 to 25°C). Spring and fall are usually cloudy, with temperatures between 46 and 59°F (8 and 15°C). Eastern Austria receives less than 31.5 inches (80 cm) of rain annually, the rest of the country between 27.6 and 78.7 inches (70 and 200 cm) a year.

In the Alps, summers are short and winters long. The sheltered valleys facing south are filled with fog and cold air, while resorts in the mountain villages enjoy warmer and cleaner air throughout the year.

The foehn is a warm, dry southerly wind that blows down the mountains of Austria in spring and fall. The same type of wind in the Rocky Mountains and Sierra Nevadas in the United States is called the chinook. It is created when moisture condenses out of the wind onto the mountains, warming the wind as it descends the slopes. This is beneficial for farmers at high altitudes who can take advantage of the warmer climate produced.

However, the foehn also causes snow to melt and slide down the mountain slopes. Sudden rushes of snow, or avalanches, pose an immediate danger to people caught in them. Big avalanches sometimes block off roads so that small mountain communities may be cut off from the rest of the country for long periods of time.

Mountain flowers.

FORESTS AND MEADOWS

Forests and woodland cover almost 40 percent of Austria. Deciduous forests of beech and oak protect mountain slopes up to about 4,000 feet (1,220 m). Fir and spruce grow above 4,000 feet (1,220 m), where the soil is thinner.

Closer to the summits, coniferous forests of pine and larch dominate, but above 6,565 feet (2,001 m), trees give way to Alpine meadows. Orchids, poppies, and edelweiss grow at these heights. These flowers are unique to the Alpine landscape, having adapted to the low temperatures, strong winds, and seasonal snows. Small and compact, Alpine plants grow near the ground. They appear soon after the snow melts in the spring to make full use of the short growing season.

Lake Neusiedler in Burgenland, the largest steppe lake in Europe, is a habitat for thick reed beds covering more than half the lake's surface.

Much previously forested land around the Alps has been turned into arable land. The Danube river valley and the eastern lowlands constitute the bulk of Austria's arable land.

FAUNA

Austrian fauna includes foxes, marten, deer, hares, badgers, squirrels, wildcats, pheasant, and partridge.

Chamois, ibex, and marmots inhabit the mountains. The chamois is an antelope with short horns that curve downward at the back. The ibex is a goat with large curved horns. The marmot, a rodent similar to the woodchuck, lives in a colony and hibernates.

Red deer and roe deer are popular targets for hunting enthusiasts. Wolves and brown bears have completely disappeared from Austria's landscape.

Birds such as the purple heron, spoonbill, and avocet are among more than 300 bird species in the reed beds on Lake Neusiedler.

The ptarmigan, rarely seen up close, lives in the Alps. Its feathers change color with the season: brown in summer, white in winter. In coldest weather, the ptarmigan huddles and allows itself to be buried under the snow until the weather improves.

A regular visitor to the Salzburg area is the griffon vulture from the Balkans. Even with its wingspan of 10 feet (3 m), the griffon vulture is not a common sight. Rarer yet is the golden eagle, which hunts with a partner over the same area all of its life.

Marine life in Austria includes fish such as salmon, char, pike, and catfish, amphibians such as the moor frog, and freshwater molluscs. The construction of power stations along the Austrian Danube has been a major threat to the river's marine life.

A red deer.

13

A cruise boat takes tourists down the Danube, past the Wachau valley, offering glimpses of castle ruins, vineyards, and orchards.

THE DANUBE

Although the Danube's path through the provinces of Upper and Lower Austria is only 217 miles (349 km), 96 percent of the country is drained by the river and its tributaries. Where the river enters Austria from Germany the scenery is dramatic, as the valleys are narrow and either thick forests or sheer cliffs loom up on either side. In this area the river drops 3 feet (1 meter) every mile (1.6 km), and the turbulent water makes it very difficult to navigate without a motorboat.

Downriver of the city of Linz, the landscape becomes more picturesque as the Danube enters the Wachau valley. Along the riverbanks, bare rocks soften into hills and dark forests yield to vineyards and orchards. Medieval castles perched on the slopes add to the romantic atmosphere. As the river approaches Vienna, it stretches out in swampy channels, but engineers have channeled the river through a canal for its passage through the city.

PROVINCES AND CITIES

Austria has nine provinces, with personalities defined by topography and economy. Vienna, the federal capital, is the commercial, industrial, and administrative heart of Austria and a province in its own right. Austria's second smallest province is Vorarlberg, at the westernmost end of the country.

Burgenland, the country's easternmost province, is predominantly agricultural, producing wheat, corn, vegetables, fruit, and wines. Lake Neusiedler, Europe's largest steppe lake, is a popular tourist attraction in Burgenland.

Carinthia, the southernmost province, has some 200 lakes, several with popular resorts. The town of Villach near the province's borders with Slovenia and Italy, is the biggest road and rail junction in the eastern Alps. Carinthia's most important natural resources are hydroelectricity and timber.

Upper Austria is the country's largest source of oil and natural gas after Lower Austria. Upper Austria draws tourists to several scenic lakes in the Salzkammergut region.

Salt gave the province of Salzburg its name; salt has been mined here for centuries. Styria, on the other hand, is frequently referred to as Austria's "green province," because half of it is covered by forests and a further quarter by grassland and vineyards. Styria is also Austria's leading mining province; the Erzberg ("ore mountain") and the town of Eisenerz ("iron ore") are located here. Austria's automobile industry is centered in the capital of Styria, Graz.

Tirol earns more foreign currency through tourism than does any other province of Austria. Tirol is situated at the junction of numerous highways. Innsbruck, its capital, hosted the Winter Olympics in 1964 and 1976.

The Danube, a river 1,770 miles (2,848 km) long flowing through much of central Europe, was once the northern frontier of the Roman empire.

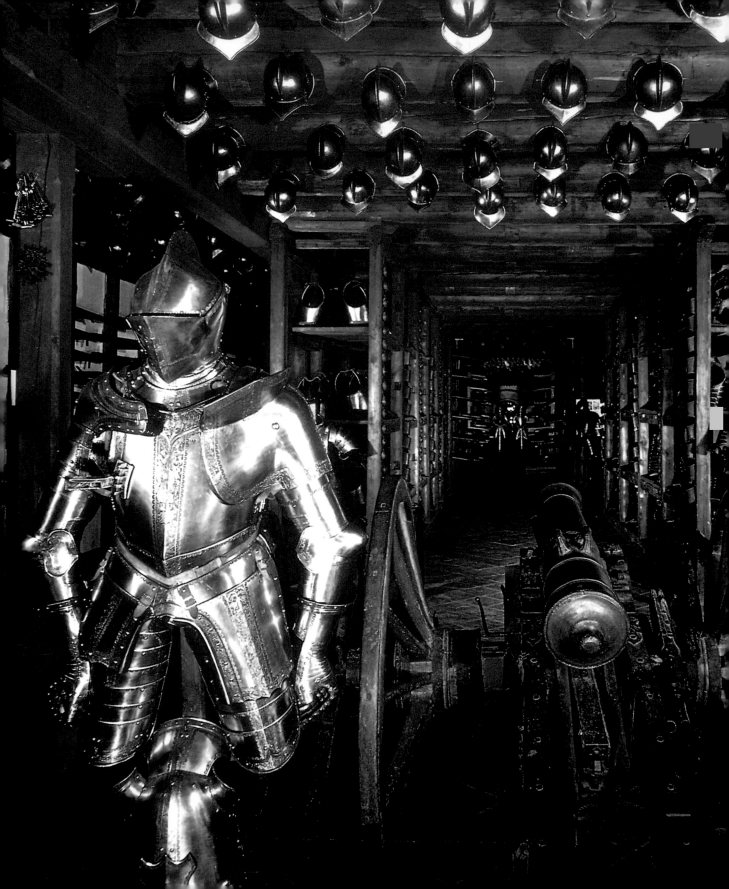

HISTORY

THE EARLIEST TRACES OF HUMAN LIFE in Austria are the remains of Neanderthal man, who is believed to have lived some 60,000 years ago. After the last Ice Age, hunter-gatherers and farmers settled in Austria's mountain valleys. It is likely that they traveled along the Danube.

From around 800 B.C., Austria grew into an important commercial center. Travelers followed the Danube valley through Austria between eastern and western Europe, and the Brenner Pass was a safe route for traders going south through the Alps to Rome or Alexandria.

From an early Celtic settlement on the banks of the Danube developed the civilization that would become a powerful European empire lasting over 600 years. Today, Austria's importance again derives from its unique location between the East and the West as post-Communist Eastern European countries look West.

Left: **Tourists in Vienna can enjoy a ride in a carriage driven by a coachman in a bowler hat.**

Opposite: **At Graz, armor, muskets, and cannon were kept ready for battle against the Turks in the 17th century.**

Vienna by the banks of the Danube. A famous 19th-century Austrian statesman, Metternich, once said, "Eastwards from Vienna, the Orient begins."

THE CELTS AND ROMANS

The Celts moved into Austria around 400 B.C., establishing the kingdom of Noricum, where they stayed for over 300 years. They opened up copper and salt mines in Austria and established a village where Vienna is today. The Celts brought to Austria their technical skills and a love of art that is characteristic of present-day Austrians.

Around 30 B.C., Roman invaders displaced the Celts. Although the Romans had explored the Danube long before, it was not until then that they made the Danube their northern frontier against the Germanic peoples who threatened their empire.

The Romans occupied Austria and set up the provinces of Raetia, Noricum, and Pannonia. They fortified the Celtic village on the banks of the Danube and named it Vindobona. Vindobona would later become Vienna.

As in other parts of Europe, the Romans built good roads and established laws that laid the foundations for the development of commerce and civic life. The Roman emperor and philosopher Marcus Aurelius spent a lot of time in Austria trying to consolidate a firm defense against the tribes of northern Europe. He died in Vindobona in A.D. 180.

Roman rule in Austria lasted four centuries. Although the first 200 years were peaceful and prosperous, later years were more turbulent.

INVASIONS AND THE HOLY ROMAN EMPIRE

Germanic tribes attacked Austria many times in the latter half of the second century A.D. After the fifth century, when the Roman armies withdrew, Austria was occupied by Germanic tribes from the north and Slavs from the east. The Asian conqueror, Attila, and his army of Huns also raided much of the Danube valley.

Salzburg Cathedral, a glorious product of European religious zeal.

Records of these centuries are scarce and the invaders were diverse. Their legacy seems minimal compared to the impact of Christianity, which began spreading in this part of Europe around the sixth and seventh centuries as missionaries from countries like Ireland spread their beliefs and established churches. In A.D. 774, a cathedral was erected in the town of Salzburg, now one of Austria's larger cities.

In A.D. 788, Austria came under the control of Charlemagne, emperor of the Germanic Franks. It was Charlemagne who gave Austria its name. He called it *Österreich* ("OOST-er-rike"), meaning Eastern Kingdom, because it was the easternmost frontier of his empire.

In the late ninth century, the Magyars of Hungary made continual raids into the Danube valley and threatened to break up Charlemagne's great empire. Otto I, a German king, finally managed to defeat the Magyars at the Battle of Lech in A.D. 955. Austria became an independent state, and in A.D. 962 the pope crowned Otto Holy Roman emperor.

Hochosterwitz Castle, a fortified limestone outcrop in Carinthia, was used as a defensive position against invaders.

THE FIRST ROYAL FAMILY

Austria's first royal family were a group of German nobles called the Babenbergs. They were originally given the land around Vienna, but extended their domain to cover much of Austria. Leopold I was the first Babenberg to be appointed *margrave* ("MAR-grave"), or provincial ruler of Austria, in A.D. 976 by Otto II, the Holy Roman emperor. The Babenberg dynasty lasted almost 300 years, during which Austria remained a part of the Holy Roman empire and the Babenbergs supported the emperor in disputes with the pope. In 1156 Austria was granted the status of a duchy by the Holy Roman emperor. This was an era of prosperity: the economy grew, the Danube became an important trade route, and Vienna became established as the capital city. According to legend, Vienna flourished because of the huge ransom paid for the release of the English king, Richard the Lionheart.

RICHARD THE LIONHEART

Toward the end of Babenberg rule, in the late 12th century, the Third Crusade took place. Although the Crusades were conducted as a religious war between Christian Europe and the Muslim Arabs, in reality they were a struggle for control of valuable trade routes through the Middle East. During the Third Crusade, the Duke of Austria had a quarrel with the English king, Richard I, also known as Richard the Lionheart.

In 1192, when Richard was returning to England after the Crusade, he tried to pass through Austria in disguise but was discovered. The duke held him prisoner in Dürnstein Castle (*below*), overlooking the Danube. Back home in England, Richard's brother, John, ruled unjustly. This was the period of the legendary Robin Hood of Sherwood Forest, a staunch supporter of Richard the Lionheart.

Legend has it that a faithful minstrel searched everywhere for the king, singing beneath every castle wall he could find. When he reached Dürnstein, Richard recognized his voice and sang along. Only after a hefty ransom was paid did the Duke of Austria release the English king. Richard the Lionheart returned triumphantly to England in 1194. But he soon left for France and never returned.

THE HAPSBURG EMPIRE

A statue of Empress Maria Theresa. The empress brought great prosperity to the Hapsburg dynasty with her reforms in the 18th century.

After the last Babenberg died with no heir, Rudolf of Hapsburg became ruler of Austria. The Hapsburg dynasty ruled Austria and large areas of Europe from 1278 to 1918. The central kingdom was around Austria, Hungary, and Bohemia. Through diplomatic marriages, the Hapsburgs added territory to their empire, which eventually stretched from Spain to Hungary.

The Hapsburg empire was so great that many wars were fought over it. In the Thirty Years War, which lasted from 1618 to 1648, Catholic Hapsburg forces fought Protestant armies from northern Europe. The greatest challenge came in the 17th century when the Turks almost captured Vienna, but they were pushed back and eventually defeated.

After Charles VI died in 1740, his daughter Maria Theresa became ruler. Others fought her on the grounds that a woman could not become ruler. Some territories were lost to the Prussians in the War of Succession, but Maria Theresa proved to be one of the greatest rulers of the Hapsburg empire. She encouraged industrial growth, lowered taxes on peasants, promoted education, and reformed the legal system.

THE EMPIRE ENDS

Austria was weakened as a result of the Napoleonic wars at the beginning of the 18th century. Nevertheless its territory still included Hungary, a part of northern Italy, and a number of German states under Austrian leadership. But in 1859 Austria lost its Italian territories and then its leadership of the German states. In 1867 Emperor Franz Josef agreed to give greater autonomy to Hungary.

In 1908 Austria-Hungary took over some of Serbia's territory. But it was not peaceful. In 1914 a Serb nationalist assassinated the heir to the Austrian throne, an event that sparked off World War I. Austria-Hungary and Germany fought on one side against the allied forces of Serbia, Italy, Russia, France, and Britain.

The Schloss Schönbrunn was the summer palace of the Hapsburgs. The design and decorations have remained as they were since the time of Empress Maria Theresa.

Austria-Hungary found itself on the losing side of World War I in 1918, and its empire was divided among the victors. The last emperor abdicated, ending 600 years of Hapsburg rule, and a new Austria, one-eighth its former size, was declared a republic.

After World War I, the Austrian economy went through a difficult time. The worldwide recession in the 1930s caused mass unemployment. Many Austrians felt that their country could not survive as a separate state due to its reduced size, and there was increasing support for a union with Germany. This almost resulted in civil war. Austrian Nazis organized a coup in 1934 to overthrow the government, but they were unsuccessful. In 1938 Germany invaded Austria and declared an *anschluss* ("ahn-SHLOOS"), or union, with Germany.

AUSTRIA IN WORLD WAR II

On March 12, 1938, German troops invaded Austria and annexed it to the German Reich. Ironically, Adolf Hitler, who was responsible for the *anschluss,* was born and brought up in Austria. Hitler left Austria when he was young. In Germany, he joined and built up the Nazi party, eventually becoming its leader.

The German invasion of Austria in 1938, a year before the outbreak of World War II, was accepted by the other European powers. But a year later, after Germany invaded Poland and Hitler's empire-building ambitions became obvious, Britain declared war.

The Nazis began a process of extermination, establishing death camps in Poland. Thousands of Austrian Jews were sent to their death in gas chambers in these camps. In Austria, the Nazis built a concentration camp near the village of Mauthausen (*above*) on the Danube; thousands were murdered here. The infamous Adolf Eichmann, one of the architects of the Holocaust, was Austrian. So too was Amon Goeth, commandant of the Plaszow concentration camp in Poland.

World War II ended in Austria in March 1945 when Allied troops captured it. Elections were held and a provisional government took over, but Austria only became fully independent in May 1955 when Allied forces withdrew from the country. Austria's traumatic wartime experiences have created a desire for peace and neutrality.

MODERN TIMES

In the late 1980s, the collapse of communism in the Soviet Union had a major impact on Austria. Many countries in Eastern Europe rejected communism. As East Germany knocked down the Berlin Wall, other Eastern bloc countries gradually overthrew their communist leaders as well. A wave of revolutions led to the collapse of the Soviet system.

This led to mass emigration of Eastern Europeans in search of a new life in the West. The influx of immigrants in Austria raised tensions among a section of the population, and the ultraconservative, anti-immigration Freedom Party under the leadership of Jörg Haider grew in popularity, leading to fears of a revival of Nazism in Austria.

The influx of refugees from the former Yugoslavia in the 1990s further fueled a fear of foreigners that prevailed among some Austrians. Haider and his party were able to exploit this fear, and Austria's international image has suffered greatly as a result.

Critics point to the fact that when Nazi Germany invaded Austria in 1938 there was no resistance, and when Hitler traveled through the country, he was greeted by enthusiastic crowds of supporters.

On the other hand, Austria was awarded a humanitarian award by a Jewish refugee organization in 1989 in recognition of the transit aid given over the years to nearly 300,000 Soviet Jews.

Present-day Austria is trying to recover from the damage inflicted on its international reputation as a result of accusations that many Austrians suffer from xenophobia—an irrational dislike and fear of foreigners—and are too willing to support racist political groups.

It has come as a shock to many Austrians to discover that their country, long portrayed as a land of music-loving citizens, is being characterized as a place of narrow-mindedness and intolerance.

After World War II, Austria was occupied by the four major nations that had defeated Nazi Germany— the United States, Britain, France, and the USSR. This occupation continued until 1955 when Austria became fully independent.

GOVERNMENT

FOR THE FIRST 50 YEARS of the last century, government in Austria was in a state of change and disorder. The arena of politics was characterized by a deep split between the conservative forces of the countryside—where the Catholic Church was powerful—and the socialist groups in the cities that demanded change and reform.

After the withdrawal of foreign troops in 1955, Austria began to rebuild its identity as an independent country with a new spirit of cooperation, determined to avoid the conflicts of the past. For a long time, Austria's political scene was regarded as dull and uneventful, but that changed considerably after the fall of the Eastern bloc, due mostly to the rise in support for conservative politicians like Jörg Haider.

An interesting feature of the constitution of the democratic Republic of Austria (passed in 1920) is that it allows for any bill to be put before the parliament for approval if it can show the support of at least 400,000 citizens. This allows petitions to be made before the parliament that do not necessarily come from one of the main parties.

Austria is a federation of nine provinces, each of which has a governor and a legislature with elected officials that can pass laws relating to the province.

Below: **The City Hall in Vienna is a Gothic-style Flemish guildhall.**

Opposite: **The Parliament Building in Vienna.**

THE FEDERAL GOVERNMENT

The government of the Republic of Austria has an executive branch, a legislative branch called the Federal Assembly, and a judicial branch headed by the Supreme Judicial Court.

THE EXECUTIVE BRANCH

The executive branch is headed by a president and chancellor. The chancellor is like a prime minister; he is the head of the government. The chancellor is the leader of the political party holding the majority of seats in the legislature. He is backed by a cabinet of ministers whom he chooses.

The federal president is the head of state. He is elected by all citizens for a period of six years. The president appoints the chancellor and is the commander-in-chief of the armed forces. In reality, the president is more of a figurehead and usually follows the suggestions of the chancellor in making important decisions.

THE FEDERAL ASSEMBLY

The bicameral Federal Assembly consists of a National Council and a Federal Council. The Federal Council consists of 64 representatives from the nine provinces. Each province elects its representatives as well as successors should the representatives be unable to complete their terms.

The federal president decides the number of representatives each province is entitled to, based on the last census.

The 183-member National Council represents the country as a whole. The National Council is the more important arm of the legislative body. While bills apart from the budget need approval from both the Federal Council and the National Council, the National Council can override a Federal Council veto by a simple majority vote.

The maximum number of representatives a province may have in the Federal Council is 12; the minimum is three.

AUSTRIA ON THE WORLD STAGE

Austria became a member of the United Nations on December 14, 1955, and has played an active role in dealing with global problems. It has been a member of numerous commissions in the United Nations, and since 1960, Austria has also contributed to peacekeeping missions all over the world.

Austria's neutrality and its geographic position in the heart of Europe are two reasons why it was picked to be one of the permanent seats of the United Nations. A number of United Nations organizations are housed in the Vienna International Center (*above*), which was opened on August 23, 1979.

Other United Nations agencies that are also located in Vienna are the International Atomic Energy Agency and the United Nations Industrial Development Organization.

Another international organization that is headquartered in Vienna is the Organization of Petroleum Exporting Countries (OPEC).

One of Austria's most important international figures was Kurt Waldheim, Secretary-General of the United Nations from 1971 to 1981. Waldheim also served as president of Austria from 1986 to 1992. However, his term as president was marred by allegations that he participated in Nazi atrocities during World War II. Waldheim denied these allegations, but even after his election as president, the allegations persisted.

In 1988 the United States put Waldheim on their list of undesirable aliens and he faced international isolation. A commission of international historians investigated the allegations and found that while there was no proof of Waldheim's personal guilt, he had nevertheless been aware of Nazi atrocities committed in the Balkans. Although this was a blow to Waldheim, he did not resign from the presidency. He carried on until his term expired in 1992.

Austrian chancellor Dr. Wolfgang Schuessel of the People's Party speaking in parliament.

POLITICAL PARTIES

The Austrian political scene is dominated by the Social Democratic Party led by Alfred Gusenbauer, the People's Party led by Wolfgang Schuessel, and the Freedom Party led by Susanne Riess-Passer. There are also the Greens, the Liberals, the Communists, and the Independents.

Until the late 1990s, elections followed a fairly predictable pattern. For many years Austrians tended to vote for one or the other of two parties. People in the cities preferred the Social Democratic Party, which had ties to the trade unions, while people in the countryside tended to vote for the People's Party, a more conservative party with links to the Catholic Church.

On average, each party had an almost equal share of votes, making it difficult for either to form a majority government that could rule effectively on its own. In practice, the two parties formed a coalition and shared the important posts.

While coalition governments in some countries tend not to survive long, with political rivalries becoming bitter and persistent, the system in Austria worked surprisingly well and the citizens were generally content with their coalition government.

The 1999 general elections, however, changed political life in Austria in a very dramatic way (although it did not bring the system of coalition governments to an end). For the first time since the 1950s, a third party gained enough votes to upset the usual result of general elections and make Austrian politics the talk of newspapers all over Europe.

THE FREEDOM PARTY

The Freedom Party campaigned in the 1999 elections with slogans like *"Stop der berfremdung. Österreich zuerst."* ("Stop the foreign tide. Put Austria first.") Jörg Haider's party took a surprising second place in the elections, gaining over 50 seats in the parliament.

In February 2000 the Social Democratic Party and the People's Party formed a new coalition government that included the Freedom Party, despite diplomatic sanctions imposed by some European Union countries.

Soon after the formation of the new coalition, Haider resigned as the leader of his party and did not take any post in the new administration.

The new leader of the Freedom Party, Susanne Riess-Passer, was not as strongly identified with extreme right-wing views and seemed more acceptable to other European nations. Diplomatic sanctions against Austria were dropped in the middle of 2000.

However, there is widespread belief that Haider's resignation was only a way of deflecting international criticism. Many Austrians, feeling that their country was being unfairly portrayed as a supporter of neo-Nazi policies, organized a public campaign called *Widerstand* ("V-der-stand"), or Resistance. They wanted to show the world that liberalism and tolerance were still core values in Austrian society.

It remains to be seen whether Haider will remain an influential figure in the Freedom Party, and more importantly, whether his party will continue to draw support from Austrians.

Former Freedom Party leader Jörg Haider.

AUSTRIA AND HUMAN RIGHTS

In 2000 a panel set up by the EU not only gave Austria's human rights record under the new government a clean bill of health, but also found Austria's treatment of minorities to be better than that in many other EU countries. According to *The Economist*'s World Human Rights Record, Austria's record serves as an example to the rest of the world.

Among rights and freedoms guaranteed to the Austrian people are: freedom of speech and the press and the right to publish in an ethnic language, freedom of religion and the right to abstain from religious education in schools, freedom of peaceful assembly and association (except for Nazi organizations), freedom to move around within the country, freedom to travel abroad and return at any time, and freedom to emigrate.

The law protects children's rights set by international conventions. The national Ministry for Youth and Family Affairs and the provincial governments employ officials to handle cases of children's rights violations. The law also protects women, the disabled, and ethnic and religious minorities from discrimination in employment and other matters.

Austrian society has an innate orderliness. After the horrors of World War II and the struggle to stabilize after the war, riots and strikes are seen as counterproductive ways to resolve disputes. The national police maintain internal security.

THE RIGHT TO VOTE

The right to change their government peacefully is a freedom guaranteed to Austrian citizens, and Austrians exercise this right by voting in periodic, free, and fair elections.

In 1986 the Austrian people voted the Social Democratic Party and the People's Party to a governing partnership that has continued since. Dr. Thomas Klestil of the People's Party was elected for a second term in the 1998 presidential election.

Austrians also have the right to vote or to stand as a candidate in elections to the European Parliament, which represents some 375 million European citizens in 15 countries. There are 21 Austrians among the more than 600 European Parliament members, who are elected every five years by direct universal suffrage through proportional representation. The first elections to the European Parliament were held in 1979.

Dr. Thomas Klestil, president of Austria since May 24, 1992.

While Austrian voters generally abide by their country's own rules during elections to the European Parliment, they share some rules with the citizens of other EU nations such as the right to vote from 18 years of age, equality for men and women, and ballot secrecy.

In 1993 a treaty was signed that gave European citizens an added right—to vote or to stand for election to the European Parliament in another member state that they have made their country of residence.

ECONOMY

THE AUSTRIAN ECONOMY IS STRONG and balanced. Industry accounts for around 30 percent of the gross domestic product (GDP), while services contribute more than 67 percent. Agriculture makes up around 2 percent of the GDP. Austria's low inflation rate of 2 percent is the envy of many countries, and the trade unions work closely with the government to minimize industrial unrest.

Since January 1995 Austria has been a member of the European Union. In January 2002 Austria adopted the common European currency, the euro.

Below: **A town square in Graz, Austria's second largest city. Population trends show a drift from the countryside to the cities for employment.**

Opposite: **A flea market in Vienna.**

A display of pottery along a wine route in southern Styria. Traditional industries are still a thriving part of Austria's modern economy.

ECONOMIC CHANGES

Austria's old currency, the schilling, is no longer accepted as legal tender. The advantage of sharing the same currency with other EU nations that have adopted the euro is that citizens of these countries can complete transactions without having to make currency exchanges. This simplifies economic life for both individuals and companies.

The Austrian economy is based mostly on private ownership, with the government operating several major companies. Government ownership of important industries goes back to the post-World War II period when government investment became necessary to rebuild a war-devastated economy. Thus the coal and oil industries, iron and steel production, and electricity generation came under government control. Now privatization is gradually reducing the government's role.

INDUSTRY

Austria's industrial sector revolves around the use of the country's natural resources. The larger industrial works are spread across the country, with the heaviest concentration of factories in the vicinity of Vienna, where approximately 20 percent of the national population live and work.

Other manufacturing areas are found near large towns like Graz, the second largest city in Austria. In Styria, important supplies of iron ore provide the basis for the steel industry. Austria also produces graphite, zinc, salt, lead, and copper, among other minerals.

After World War II, extensive programs were implemented to develop heavy industries such as hydroelectric power generation, oil, natural gas, chemicals, mining, and textiles. While these programs have helped to bolster a prosperous and fairly stable economy, they have also resulted in a change in the country's character and traditions. More and more Austrians, especially the younger generation, now leave the countryside for the cities in search of employment.

In Vienna, factories producing cars, locomotives, and other vehicles employ a large number of people. Other major sources of employment are food-processing factories, textile and clothing factories, and plants that manufacture furniture, paper and pulp, optical instruments, and porcelain and glass products.

Austria prides itself on manufacturing quality rather than mere quantity. Many of the country's factories count the number of their employees in the hundreds rather than in the thousands. Products that Austria is famous for, such as quality glassware, porcelain, and jewelry, require the input of highly-skilled craftspeople more than that of assembly-line workers.

A corn harvest. Harvesting is still done by hand on mountain farms where the slopes are too steep for machines.

FORESTRY AND AGRICULTURE

Much of Austria's cultivated land is used for forestry. Spruce and other conifers are planted, left to mature, and then cut down for commercial use. Reforestation is ongoing so there is little of the original forest that once carpeted much of central Europe. A lot of timber is exported untreated. Timber processed within the country is turned into paper for export.

Most farms in Austria are family-run and usually smaller than 52 acres (21 hectares). For many, agriculture is a part-time concern; tourism provides their primary source of income. Farmers rent out rooms or work as mountain guides or ski instructors in popular tourist areas like Tirol. In regions bordering the Czech Republic, Slovakia, Hungary, and Slovenia, there is little tourism and the farming population is dwindling.

Since mountain slopes are not friendly to modern machinery and tourism offers farmers better financial benefits, the government gives out subsidies to mountain farmers in an effort to preserve mountain farming and the cultural landscape in the Alps.

Although less than 20 percent of Austria's land is suitable for growing crops, 75 percent of its food supply comes from its farms. Among the crops grown are potatoes, wheat, barley, corn, sugar beets, rye, oats, and fruit such as grapes for wine. Since grass and clover grow well, most Alpine farmers also rear cattle. There are even pipelines to transport milk from highland farms to points in the valleys below.

Austria has a reputation for brewing high-quality lager. There are small breweries that dominate their local areas and also large national companies that produce specialty beers such as *Weissbier* ("VISE-beer"), a fizzy wheat beer. Austrian white wine is world-famous. Burgenland produces most of Austria's red wine.

Nearly all farmers in Austria breed cattle. The cows graze on the grass and clover that grow so well in the pastures.

A ski pulley in Kirchdorf. Austria's ski resorts attract thousands of tourists each year.

TOURISM—BLESSING OR BLIGHT?

Tourism is vitally important to the Austrian economy. In 2000 more than 17.8 million tourists visited Austria, more than twice the country's population of 8.1 million. Most visitors to Austria come from Western Europe, mainly Germany (perhaps attracted by the common language), followed by the Netherlands and Britain.

Tourism today adds more than $1 billion to Austria's annual national income. The mountain resorts draw visitors all year round. The top three cities tourists visit are: Vienna, the country's capital; Salzburg, with its world-famous music festivals and romantic architecture; and Innsbruck, beautifully situated amid mountains.

For scenic beauty, popular tourist destinations are the provinces of Tirol, Salzburg, Carinthia, and Vienna, and the country's lake district, Salzkammergut southeast of Salzburg.

The effect of tourism can be seen in the way new houses are built in the western provinces. An extra floor is added for the purpose of renting rooms to visitors. The price to pay for such large-scale tourism is the change in the social structure of valley life in these regions. Some people feel that customs and traditions are trivialized and their cultural meaning lost when they are commercialized for the tourism industry.

ENVIRONMENTAL CONCERNS

NUCLEAR POWER In 1986 Austria experienced severe contamination by radioactive fallout following the Chernobyl nuclear disaster in the former Soviet Union. Thousands of tons of food had to be destroyed. The disaster also settled controversy over the future of Austria's Zwentendorf nuclear plant. This plant had been completed in 1978 but was never opened because of opposition within Austria to nuclear power. After the Chernobyl disaster, the plant was dismantled piece by piece and sold to anyone who wanted spare parts for a nuclear power station.

In the mid-1980s Germany's plans to build a large nuclear reprocessing plant in Wackersdorf in Bavaria drew massive protest not only in Germany but also from Austria. Construction of the facility was abandoned in 1989.

WILDLIFE PROTECTION Austria has the largest primeval riverine forest in the whole of Europe—the Hainburg Forest north of Burgenland at 31 square miles (80 square km). For almost a decade, the stretch of the Danube near the Hainburg lay under threat as proposals were made to build a large hydroelectric plant, raising concern that it would destroy as much as 10 percent of the forest and prevent the annual spring flooding of the rest of the forest. Supporters of the project argued

that the plant would mean fewer fossil-fueled power stations and less acid rain. Critics pointed out that if the Danube ceased to flow through and be cleansed by the forest, the groundwater that Vienna depended on would become polluted.

In 1996, 38.6 square miles (100 square km) of the forest were officially declared the Danube Flood Plain National Park. In 1997 the park gained international recognition as a protected area.

Conservation programs started to preserve eastern Austria's wetlands have led to the protection of many birds such as storks (*right*).

ENVIRONMENT

A HIGHLY INDUSTRIALIZED COUNTRY, Austria shares responsibility with other major industrial nations for the effects of pollution on the natural environment.

At home, the government has taken action to moderate the impact of tourism and industrialization on nature and to develop programs that enable people to live in a way that supports conservation efforts. The government encourages environmental awareness by widening public access to information and monitoring public concerns.

Recognizing that environmental protection is a global challenge, Austria has joined in international efforts to effectively address urgent issues such as global warming. For example, Austria is part of the International Commission for the Protection of the Alps (CIPRA), which seeks to preserve the natural and cultural heritage of the Alps.

Left: **Lüner Lake in Brandner Valley in Vorarlberg.**

Opposite: **A forest creek in Bregenzerwald.**

CONSERVATION

Forests are important in helping to prevent avalanches, floods, and soil erosion. The Austrian government is aware that ongoing large-scale replanting programs are necessary if the country's forests are to be preserved. Austria practices reforestation for trees with commercial uses. Replanted spruce and fir, for example, are harvested for the production of paper as well as to supply lumber to the construction industry.

Forest conservation laws are also in place. Austria's Forestry Act, enacted more than 25 years ago, sets out the rules for planting new trees whenever existing ones are cut down.

The alpine meadows are home to a colorful variety of flowers found nowhere else. The small white edelweiss, a typical alpine flower made famous by the film *The Sound of Music*, is a highly protected flower; it is strictly against the law to pick it.

There are also laws for the protection of endangered animals. The chamois, for example, could disappear completely from the Austrian landscape unless given rigorous protection. The Danube, once brimming with more than 70 species of fish, is losing its diversity of marine life due to pollution. It is possible that the giant catfish, for instance, which is capable of growing up to 13 feet (4 m) in length, will one day cease to swim Austria's waters.

NATIONAL PARKS

About a third of Austria's forested land—around 4,315 square miles (11,177 square km)—has been officially declared as protected. Some 50 ancient woodland areas have been designated as natural reserves protected by law.

Austria's first national park, Hohe Tauern, was established in 1981. Covering approximately 695 square miles (1,800 square km) in western Austria, the park straddles the provinces of Carinthia, Salzburg, and Tirol and includes Austria's highest mountain, the Grossglockner. In 2001 the International Union for Conservation of Nature (IUCN) granted Hohe Tauern international status as a national park.

Other national parks in Austria include the Neusiedlersee–Seewinkle, a habitat for a wide variety of bird life, and the Donauauen, or Danube Flood Plain National Park.

THE IMPACT OF GLOBAL WARMING ON AUSTRIA

Global warming is melting Alpine glaciers and hurting European winter tourism. The economic consequences are nowhere more alarming than in Austria, where most of the country's skiing activity takes place at altitudes of less than 3,281 feet (1,000 m) above sea level. Snow at these heights is especially susceptible to temperature increases. As the Alps warm up and snow lines recede (possibly by as much as 1,968 feet, or 600 m, within 15 years), many low-level resorts in Austria may in the future receive no snow and have to shut down.

The consequences of this global environmental problem for the Austrian economy will be dramatic as skiers spend their winter vacations elsewhere, jobs are lost, and national income decreases (no other country is as dependent on skiing).

The intensity and timing of Alpine snowfall are changing, resulting in short heavy falls and causing avalanches among other problems. Scientists have found with satellite imaging that the Po valley and the region around the Alps in Austria, Germany, and Switzerland are receiving less snow cover than in the past. At Austria's lower-altitude resorts, lost days at the start and end of winter mean shorter ski seasons that cut Christmas and Easter tourist traffic.

At higher altitudes, however, more snow is falling later than usual. Thus the skiing season is stretching into spring. Higher-level resorts such as Obertauern (*below*) at 5,250 feet (1,600 m) may stand a better chance of drawing vacationers venturing higher in search of thicker snow cover.

ECOTOURISM

The people of the Bregenzerwald region in Vorarlberg make a large part of their living from tourism. Their biggest challenge is to balance between marketing their home to tourists and preserving nature's gifts.

Bregenzerwald has established a regional initiative called Nature and Life that seeks to develop an eco-friendly tourism industry and a socially responsible lifestyle by maintaining symbiotic relationships among nature, people, and technology.

Communities in the region have a long tradition of cooperation. Retaining their old lifestyle, language, and clothing, they have managed to preserve their natural environment while supporting a healthy economy with its lively handicraft industry.

Bregenzerwald's efforts were featured among several projects from around the world at the World Expo 2000 in Hannover, Germany. The region was recognized for finding a formula for sustainable development that combines environmental conservation, economic self-sufficiency, and cultural and social needs.

In 2001 Austria, together with the UN Environment Program and the World Tourism Organization, held a conference in Salzburg ahead of the UN International Year of Ecotourism and International Year of Mountains 2002. The conference discussed a variety of topics concerning ecotourism in mountain areas such as managing and navigating the landscape, strategies for mountain ecotourism in Europe and around the world, and cooperation among leaders in tourism, the environment, and traffic.

The Bregenzerwald train takes tourists through the beautiful northern Alps.

KEEPING CLEAN

From 4 million tons in 1970, the volume of freight transported through Austria rose to 34.7 million tons at the end of the 20th century. More than a million trucks lumber across the Brenner Pass every year, emitting soot particles into the air.

Activists in Tirol have held protests at the Brenner Pass against truck traffic over the Alps. There have also been demands to increase rail transportation in preference to freight trucks.

The government has responded by limiting the size of international trucks crossing the country, especially via the Brenner Pass, and by looking to the rail system as a cleaner alternative for moving freight.

Another major environmental concern in Austria is tourism. Tirol, for example, receives millions of visitors every year. But the region's thriving

The Brenner Pass.

Electric boats at Wolf-
gang Lake.

tourist industry has reduced the supply of fresh water for its resident population of 640,000 and generated enormous amounts of waste.

Southern Tirol has formulated a water policy that seeks to protect its water sources from pollution and to build treatment facilities and more drains. The region has a twofold approach to waste management—disposal, which includes recycling, and reduction of waste. Not only environmental protection measures are needed to achieve this, but also efforts to increase public awareness of environmental problems. For example, basic education in Austria's elementary schools includes the cultivation of environmental consciousness.

Tirol also offers incentives to hotels that meet high standards in waste disposal and in conserving water and energy. Some farming areas control the environmental impact of tourist activities by, for example, confining them to designated areas.

Austria keeps clean in energy generation as well. Some 70 percent of the country's electricity production comes from hydroelectric plants.

AUSTRIANS

A SURE WAY TO OFFEND an Austrian is to reason that since Austria is geographically so close to Germany and Austrians speak German all the time, Austrians are "sort of Germans really." "No!" will be the Austrian's strong and immediate response. Austrians are proud of their independent identity and are acutely conscious of not being German.

Another assumption Austrians will find annoying is that they are all basically the same. A Viennese will tell you that he or she is as different from someone who lives in Vorarlberg as cheese is from stone, and the person from Vorarlberg will readily agree. Yet both will emphatically assert that they are Austrians.

Left: **People in a park. Austrian society, reflecting a divisive political history, is less homogenous than many outsiders believe.**

Opposite: **Men in Salzburg wearing their traditional clothes.**

REGIONAL DIFFERENCES

Austria is a federation of nine provinces, many of which have their own distinct character. People from Vienna are different in some ways than people from Tirol or Salzburg or Carinthia or Burgenland. Identifying someone simply as Austrian ignores their unique regional traits.

A couple in a park. Austrians living near the border may dress and behave a lot like people in a neighboring country.

The most important factor accounting for these variations is Austria's landlocked location and its proximity to so many other countries. This has in the past led to population shifts and cultural "invasions," the legacies of which significantly determine the traits that distinguish one part of Austria from another today.

Austria's geography also influenced its cultural development. The physical barriers created by the Alps nurtured cultural differences across regions and even across small communities. Austrians from one valley settlement, for example, may dress differently and

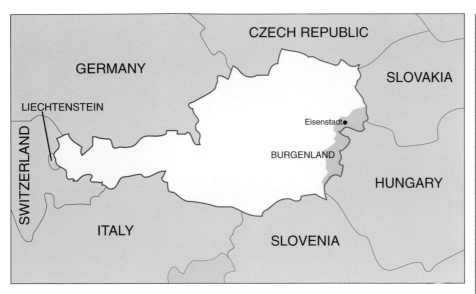

speak a different dialect from Austrians in another town or village a few miles away.

BURGENLANDERS

Burgenland is the least visited region of Austria. Its capital is Eisenstadt. Being close to Hungary has meant that the people of Burgenland, or Burgenlanders, have been exposed to Hungarian culture more than people in any other part of Austria have been.

Burgenland is one of only two regions in Austria where German is not the common language. An important Croatian minority lives among the 300,000 Burgenlanders, and Croat is the preferred language.

Historically, Burgenlanders have closer links with Hungary than with Austria. In the breakup of the Austro-Hungarian empire after World War II, a plebiscite to decide between autonomy or affiliation resulted in a slice of Hungary (now Burgenland) becoming a part of Austria.

Burgenland does not look typically Austrian. There are no snowy mountains, and the people are mostly fruit and vegetable farmers. Their produce is seasonal, reaping profits in the spring and summer but not during the winter. Without tourism to supplement their living, many Burgenlanders head for other parts of the country. There are significant numbers of Burgenland construction workers employed in Vienna.

Father and son horse-taxi drivers. Not all who work in the city were born here. Many came from the countryside to seek employment.

A farmhouse in Styria.

STYRIANS

Some 1.2 million people live in Styria. Their capital, Graz, is Austria's largest city after Vienna. Living near Slovenia, Hungary, and Italy might explain Styrians' strong sense of independence. A writer once recounted how at a farmhouse near Graz, he found out that the lamb and wine he was having for dinner were both local produce. He asked the farmer why such good-quality meat and wine were not available in the national capital, Vienna, which imports lamb from New Zealand. The farmer replied that Styrians did not *export* their lamb and wine. Selling his province's produce to his own country's capital was to him international trade!

Styrians who are not farmers are likely to be engaged in work related to one of the province's major industries: forestry, glass manufacturing, and the magnesite and iron and steel industries. Styria is the leading mining province in the nation, and its mining and steel industries have their scientific center in the Minnig University in Leoben, north of Graz.

ICEMAN OF THE ALPS

In 1991 climbers discovered the body of a man frozen in a glacier in the Oetz valley in the Alps on the Austrian-Italian border. This type of discovery is usually the body of a recent avalanche victim. But the Oetz find was different in more ways than one.

The man lying under the ice was clutching an ax and beside him lay a knife, flint, and a quiver of arrows. While some scientists speculated that the body could have been up to 500 years old, glacier specialists said it was unlikely for a glacier to be able to preserve a body that long. So well-preserved was this particular discovery that it still had skin and muscle tissue. The skeleton was complete and the head and back showed signs of violent injuries.

At the University of Innsbruck, it was claimed that the body was 4,000 years old and from the Bronze Age. Later, however, it was determined to be 5,300 years old, since the man's ax was actually made from copper.

Oetzi, as Austrians call the frozen man, is the best-preserved Stone Age man in the world. How had he been preserved so long in ice? One suggestion is that he had been mummified by freezing air before he fell into the glacier.

Oetzi is believed to have been around 46 years old and about 5.2 feet (1.6 m) tall. His clothes were made from animal skins and tree bark. Near him were found chamois hairs, pieces of birchbark sewn together, a wooden backpack, a stone necklace, and a leather pouch.

While earlier research showed that Oetzi was a vegetarian, studies carried out later on the contents of his colon, or large intestine, revealed not just cereal grains but also ibex muscle fibers. The many theories as to the cause of his death include battle, ritual sacrifice, and starvation.

The dispute between the authorities of Austria and Italy over whose territory Oetzi had been discovered on continued until 1998. Then, after six years at the University of Innsbruck, Oetzi was taken to Italy. He now lies in a chamber at 21.2°F (-6°C) and 98 percent humidity in the South Tirol Museum of Archaeology in Bolzano. The Italians call Oetzi Hibernatus.

TIROLEANS

Scenic Innsbruck, with the old quarter in the foreground and the Alps in the back. Many Tiroleans work in the tourist industry.

Around 700,000 Austrians live in an area of nearly 5,000 square miles (12,950 square km) surrounded by majestic mountains. This is Tirol, the most visited region of Austria. Its capital, Innsbruck, is the most historic and renowned city after Vienna.

Tourism is vitally important for the people of Tirol, many of whom earn their living as hoteliers and mountain guides. The tourist industry has perhaps strengthened Tirol's image as a land dominated by old farmhouses among Alpine peaks and forests.

Tiroleans have retained a lot of their traditional ways such as wearing their colorful folk clothing when performing folk dances. In a popular Tirolean courtship dance, the man stamps his heels and slaps his knees as he circles his partner. Sometimes the male dancer may do somersaults and cartwheels and jump over the female dancer.

The village of Alpbach, about 37 miles (60 km) east of Innsbruck, sits on a plateau at an altitude of 3,281 feet (1,000 m). Already "Austria's most beautiful village," in 1993 Alpbach won the title "Europe's most beautiful flower village." Alpbach has a population of 2,300 people.

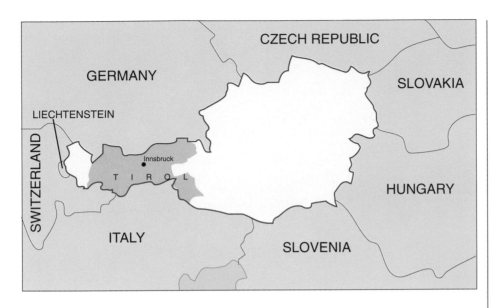

Famous for their traditions and nationalist fervor, Tiroleans are proud of their rich heritage as free and independent farmers who were never serfs to local nobility. Today, this history accounts for their strong sense of being Tirolean as well as Austrian.

This identity is connected with the turbulent history of a province that has been fought over many times. The existence of silver mines plus the proximity of the Brenner Pass through the Alps to Italy made Tirol a much disputed area. When Napoleon gave Tirol to the king of Bavaria in the early 19th century, Tiroleans rose in revolt under the leadership of Andreas Hofer, who became an important folk hero.

Some Tiroleans own property in an area in northern Italy known as South Tirol, which they believe should be a part of Austria. Post-World War I agreements gave South Tirol to Italy. During the 1960s, this became a controversial issue that led to terrorist attacks, as German-speakers in South Tirol felt that their Austrian heritage was not being given due recognition.

South Tiroleans today have some degree of autonomy and speak German.

A Tirolean farmer drives his horse cart through the village. Traditional means of transportation are still used in the countryside.

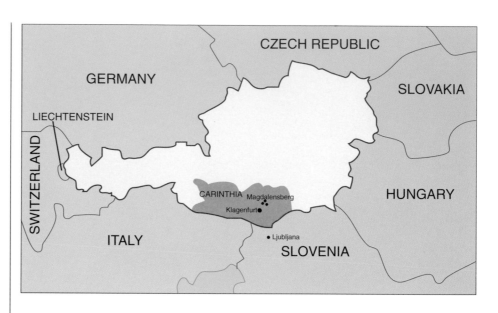

CARINTHIANS

Like Burgenlanders, Carinthians do not speak German. The minority language, Slovene, is spoken by the descendants of Slovenes who settled in the area centuries ago.

After World War I, when part of Hungary became Austria's and part of Tirol became Italy's, Austria had to also give parts of Carinthia to Italy and the then new nation of Yugoslavia. Today, many visitors to the Slovene capital of Ljubljana ("LOO-blee-AH-nah") comment on the Austrian feel of that city.

Carinthia has a rich Celtic background. Europe's largest Celtic settlement, excavated at Magdalensberg, is an important archeological site.

There are well over half a million Carinthians today, mostly farmers and mine workers. Cattle and sheep raising, corn, wheat, and fruit farming, and lignite, lead, and iron mining are major industries in Carinthia. There are plants manufacturing chemicals and textiles in both Klagenfurt, the capital of Carinthia, and Villach, an important industrial town and a major junction in the eastern Alps.

A small timber mill in Carinthia.

PEOPLE OF VORARLBERG

The German spoken in Vorarlberg sounds more like Swiss German than it does the Austrian German heard in most parts of the country, which is not that surprising when one considers that Zurich, the capital of Switzerland, is only an hour's drive away compared to a day's drive to Vienna. This most westerly province, and the second smallest in the country, is bordered by the Arlberg range in the east and opens into Switzerland and Germany in the west and north.

Both the Swiss and the people of Vorarlberg are descended from the ancient German Alemannic tribes that dominated central Europe in the third century B.C. This is why the people of Vorarlberg have a dialect that is quite distinct from the German spoken elsewhere in Austria.

Vorarlberg has a population of 350,000 people, living mostly on the plains of the Rhine. The capital of this region is Bregenz. Vorarlberg is the most traditional province of Austria. The people are proud of the customs that are uniquely theirs, especially in the Bregenzerwald region, where people continue to live much as they did in the past.

Another characteristic that unites the people in Vorarlberg is a love of nature that drives them to seek ways to live in harmony with the environment.

THE VIENNESE

Vienna is home to over 20 percent of the country's population. There are also significant Czech and Slovak communities and a large group of foreign workers, mostly from Slovenia.

The stereotype of the Viennese citizen is an elegant, sophisticated, artistic lover of classical music and cream pastries, who studies the newspaper for hours in a smart coffee house. As with so many aspects of Austrian culture, the explanation for this lies in history.

The Austrian empire came to a sudden end after World War I, but imperial attitudes did not die as quickly. Vienna, the capital city of the former empire, had taken on a rich cosmopolitan character. It was the city most patronized by artists and intellectuals, and even its ordinary citizens had a sense of being the aristocrats of Austria.

The remnants of Austria's imperial past have lived on into the 21st

A little girl dressed up to go to a wedding.

Couples dance to the music of a live orchestra at an opera ball in Vienna.

century in the Viennese "attitude," which a farmer from Vorarlberg might dismiss as snobbery. But Viennese refer to *Landl* ("LAHND-uhl"), their name for Vorarlberg meaning "the little province," in a semiaffectionate way, for there is a big-city air in their perception of the agricultural province so far west.

The city's grand architecture is another manifestation of the people's attitude. The Imperial Hofburg Palace, for example, occupies a large area in the old city and houses several museums.

The legacy of the past can also be seen in the Viennese telephone directory. One regularly comes across foreign-sounding names that are obviously not German. Viennese are proud of their rich cultural heritage. Most families in Vienna can claim a grandparent or great-grandparent of Czech or Hungarian descent.

Sigmund Freud found that the analysis of dreams brought to the surface things that a person had unconsciously repressed.

FAMOUS AUSTRIANS

SIGMUND FREUD (1856–1939) Freud is the most famous psychologist of all time. He put forward the now commonly accepted idea of the "unconscious," powerful feelings and instincts not consciously sensed that determine our behavior, especially irrational or odd behavior. Freud published his theories in books that described the dreams and fears of his patients.

Freud was born in Czechoslovakia but lived most of his life in Vienna. Being Jewish, Freud left Vienna when the Nazis came in 1938 and sent Jews to prison camps. Freud died in London the following year.

LUDWIG WITTGENSTEIN (1889–1951) Wittgenstein was one of the most influential philosophers of the 20th century. *Tractatus Logico-Philosophicus* (1922), the only book he published during his lifetime, explains through a series of short, numbered paragraphs his thinking on the limits of logic and language. The main message of the 75-page *Tractatus* in Wittgenstein's words is that "what can be said at all can be said clearly, and what we cannot talk about we must pass over in silence."

His other great works, published posthumously, were: *Philosophical Investigations* (1953), his masterpiece, written in aphorisms; and *On Certainty* (1969), which compiles his work from his last years.

Wittgenstein was born in Vienna, lived in Norway and Ireland before serving in the Austrian army during World War I, and later became a professor of philosophy at Cambridge, where he died of prostate cancer.

The Art History Museum in Vienna houses fine art collections and priceless Habsburg antiques.

OSKAR KOKOSCHKA (1886–1980) The paintings of Kokoschka, one of the great 20th-century artists, are famous for their humanist themes, intense landscapes, and fluid colors. Although Kokoschka traveled often, he always returned to Vienna where he grew up. However, his socialist convictions and outspoken criticisms of society earned him the hatred of the Nazis. Kokoschka was not Jewish, but knowing that he would never survive under the Nazi regime, he fled Vienna.

The Austrian flag with the coat of arms.

SOCIAL PARTNERSHIP

Social partnership is the term that describes the voluntary cooperation between employers and employees practiced in Austria. Trade union representatives meet behind closed doors with leaders of industry and commerce, and they thrash out matters of policy concerning changes in wages and prices. These meetings have no legal or constitutional basis, but compromises made at these meetings filter through to parliament and influence the decisions made there.

This social partnership reflects a new attitude toward economic and social life that emerged after World War II, and it is characteristic of the Austrian way of doing things. Issues that could lead to confrontation and bitterness are avoided, and compromise is seen as the best way of dealing with problems.

FACTS (AND FIGURES) OF LIFE IN AUSTRIA

Birth rate	9.74 births to every 1,000 persons
Death rate	9.8 deaths to every 1,000 persons
Fertility rate	1.39 babies to every woman
Infant mortality rate	4.44 deaths to every 1,000 live births
Life expectancy at birth	77.84 years
Population growth rate	0.24 percent
Age structure	0–14 years 16.6 percent
	15–64 years 68 percent
	65 years and older 15.4 percent
Sex ratio	1 male to 1.05 females
Hospital beds	1 bed to every 91 persons

THE COFFEEHOUSE

The coffeehouse is not just a place for drinking coffee. Coffee drinking is a way of life for Austrians, whose love of coffee dates to the end of the 17th century and the Turkish attack on Vienna. As the defeated Turks retreated in a hurry, they left behind hundreds of sacks filled with coffee beans. The Viennese initially had no idea what the brown beans were. It was an Austrian merchant who had traveled to Turkey who realized what could be done with them. He opened the first coffeehouse and experimented with the beans until he found a taste that the citizens could not resist.

The Viennese coffeehouse is now a national institution. A typical cross-section of the capital's citizens will visit a coffeehouse during the course of the day. Office workers pop in for breakfast, students sit for hours with their textbooks, businesspeople talk shop, and shoppers stop by for a break.

Regular patrons will have their own table, such as newspaper addicts who systematically work their way through the racks of national and international publications provided for customers.

Customers may order coffee once or several times, and the waiters keep serving fresh glasses of water unless another drink is ordered.

A waitress clears the table at an outdoor café.

Customers enjoy coffee and cake at the famous Sacher Hotel's coffeehouse in Vienna.

THE HEURIGER

The *heuriger* ("HI-ree-geh") is a unique kind of wine tavern commonly found in Vienna and eastern Austria. The word means "this year's," so strictly speaking only new wines are served. This is indicated by a sprig of fir or pine or a wreath of holly placed over the door of the tavern.

Inside, Austrians sit around tables talking about both crucial and trivial matters with equal enthusiasm. There is usually both hot and cold food available buffet-style. In the larger *heuriger*, especially in the tourist areas, live music is played.

Visiting a *heuriger* is unlike visiting a wine bar in the United States. A visit to a *heuriger* is often a family occasion, when children and even pets are welcome. The wine may be served mixed with soda water; this is known as a *g'spritzter* ("ges-SHPRIT-zer"). With plenty of food available, it is not unusual for a group of friends to stay chatting and socializing all evening and night.

About 800 families grow grapes for wine in the area around Vienna, and some 500 taverns pour out 12 million glasses of wine every year.

LIFE IN THE COUNTRYSIDE

Many rural families in Tirol live in farmhouses that belonged to their ancestors. The farmhouse is typically made from stone and wood, with a bell tower to summon the men from the fields at lunchtime.

Roman Catholicism is more deeply ingrained in the countryside than in the cities. A crucifix on the farmhouse gable is common, or a painted inscription above the door, "We appreciate the good that Jesus Christ has done for us."

A typical farm occupies about 2,178,000 square feet (202,343 square m) of woodland and pasture for half a dozen cows, several calves, a few pigs, and a dozen or more hens. The cows are taken up into the Alps to graze in the summer and brought down again in late autumn.

Rural Austrians in the past spent harsh Alpine winters repairing tools, living off cheese and dried meat, and making handicrafts. The animals were kept indoors and fed hay.

Tourism now offers alternative employment during the winter months, especially in western Austria. Many farmers supplement their income with money spent by tourists. They convert the living room into a bedroom, and the kitchen takes over as the center of family life during the winter months. Then when the tourists leave, farming begins again—farming families loosen the soil and plant potatoes and corn.

Some families still make cheese, although it is probably the grandparents who possess the skill. Breadmaking is more common; a simple lunch can be made out of rye bread, or *roggenbrot* ("ROGGEN-broht"). After Mass every Sunday, the men may play a card game of *watten* ("VAH-tehn"), over a jug of beer at the local beerhall.

Austrian students on a school trip to the Schloss Schönbrunn.

EDUCATION

School is compulsory in Austria, and all schools are coeducational. Every child between 6 and 10 years of age attends a *volksschule* ("folks-SHOO-leh"), or elementary school. After that, some 80 percent of elementary school students are directed into *hauptschulen* ("howpt-SHOO-len"), or general secondary schools. The remaining minority enrol in the more prestigious *allgemeinbildende höhere schulen* ("AHL-geh-mine-BIL-dent-deh HOE-heh-reh SHOO-len"), or upper-level secondary schools.

All students take English as a second language. After elementary education it is also possible to pursue vocational training by attending the medium-level or higher-level technical schools. Students attend these schools for careers in fields such as industry, agriculture, forestry, nursing, tourism, and social work.

From either an upper-level technical school or the *Allgemeinbildende Höhere Schulen* (AHS), students can enter one of the 12 universities and six art colleges in the country. Many of Austria's universities have a long history. The University of Vienna, for example, was founded in 1365, and this makes it the oldest university in German-speaking Europe. Universities in Graz and Innsbruck were founded in the 16th and 17th centuries

respectively. Graz and Vienna boast prestigious technical universities.

There are equal opportunities for all Austrians to receive an education. Children of foreign workers have the same right to free education as Austria-born children. Every student has access to free textbooks and free transportation to and from school.

SOCIAL SECURITY

A street musician in jester's clothes.

Austria has one of the best social welfare systems in the world. Compulsory national health insurance covers the medical expenses of visits to

the doctor or stays in a hospital. Similarly, workers are protected against financial loss in the event of sickness or an accident.

Social insurance also covers the self-employed, including farmers. Street entertainers can also be considered self-employed, although some sociologists call what they do disguised begging.

Unemployment benefits average nearly half the previous normal earnings, although such benefits are not paid out indefinitely. Even in the case of death, benefits include a contribution to funeral expenses.

Inevitably the system may be exploited by people who can take care of themselves financially. Stories of social security "scroungers" are often heard at the *heuriger*.

There are 13 legal holidays in the Austrian calendar, and workers receive five weeks paid vacation each year. The elderly are very well taken care of. Retired Austrians are entitled to old-age pensions. Men retire at age 65; women at age 60. The disabled also receive pensions, regardless of age.

All these benefits are financed by a combination of employers' and employees' contributions plus government funds. With more than a quarter of the proceeds of its economic growth paying for social security, Austria can justly claim to be one of the most advanced of welfare states.

A senior citizens' home in Salzburg.

THE AUSTRIAN LIFE CYCLE

In a country where 84 percent of the population are Roman Catholics, baptism is one of the earliest rites of passage for the individual. Parents bring their babies to the church where the priest performs a simple ceremony to initiate the baby into the Roman Catholic faith. Relatives and friends attend the ceremony to witness the event.

Marriage for practicing Catholics is a church affair. After the wedding ceremony, the couple leave on their honeymoon, which often means a visit to another European country, if the couple can afford it.

Funerals are church affairs as well. Before the day of the funeral, the body is laid at rest for family and friends to pay their last respects. On the day of the funeral, a ceremony is held in the church, followed by a ceremony at the graveyard as the coffin is lowered into the ground.

In the countryside, where old traditions and customs have survived relatively intact, there are rites originating in the passing of the seasons: the end of winter and the advent of spring is marked by carnivals and processions, and during the fall, there are thanksgiving ceremonies and country fairs.

Some parades still observed today have their origins in pre-Christian times. For example, during the "ghosts' parade," men dressed in costumes and large wooden masks glide through the streets in an eerie procession—a throwback to the days of pagan spirit worship.

A graveyard. Ninety percent of Austrian funerals are held in a church.

TRADITIONAL DRESS

The most characteristic Austrian traditional dress for women is the *dirndl* ("DURN-duhl"), consisting of an embroidered blouse with a lace bodice worn over a full skirt and an apron. Men wear *lederhosen* ("LAY-der-HOH-sen"), or leather shorts, with ornamental suspenders and belts. They also wear distinctive hats and short jackets without lapels.

Austrians now generally wear their traditional clothes only for festive and tourist occasions. They maintain the authentic uniqueness of their traditional dress by observing the strict regional differences in individual items. The style of the hats, for example, varies not just from one region to another but even from one valley to another. Headgear for women is sometimes very distinctively braided with gold. A woman's hat from Vorarlberg, instead of resting on the head, rises from it and looks as if it is being worn upside down.

Traditional clothes in the Salzkammergut region in central Austria resemble those of 18th-century European ladies and gentlemen, with the men donning long jackets and white socks pulled up to the knee and tied with a colored ribbon.

Almabtrieb ("ALM-ahb-treeb") is a festival where the cows are brought down from the mountain pastures. People wear their traditional clothes for this festival.

RELIGION

AUSTRIA IS A PREDOMINANTLY ROMAN CATHOLIC country, with 84 percent of the population professing that faith. Protestants make up 6 percent of the population, 4 percent follow other faiths, and 6 percent profess no religion.

Church and State were one until the fall of the Hapsburg empire; they are now separate, and divorce and abortion are legally possible even though the Church does not allow it. Roman Catholicism is traditionally practiced in the countryside more than in the cities, where people who profess to be Roman Catholic might not necessarily observe the religion strictly in their daily lives.

While regular attendance at Mass is falling, 70 percent of Austrians still marry in church, 90 percent have their children baptized, and 90 percent of funerals are held in a church.

Left: **Worshipers light candles in St. Stephen's Cathedral.**

Opposite: **Inside the Stiftskirche, a 12th-century church in Tirol.**

ROMAN CATHOLICISM

Christianity came to Austria during the time of the Roman empire. By the third century A.D., it had spread widely. Austria's Roman Catholic roots can be traced back to missionaries who founded monasteries in the fifth and sixth centuries. In the seventh century, a diocese founded at Salzburg and another at Passau became centers for the Christianization of southern and eastern Austria. Between the 10th and 13th centuries, many monasteries were founded with the encouragement of Austria's rulers. The major monastic orders were the Augustinians, Benedictines, Premonstratensians, and Cistercians. Much later, in the 16th century, other religious orders included the Jesuits, Capuchins, Barnabites, and Servites.

Catacomb in the rock, St. Peter's Cemetery in Salzburg. Carvings that depict the stations of the cross—the events leading to the crucifixion of Jesus Christ—are placed around the inside perimeter of the church. At designated times of the week, worshipers stop at each tableau to pray.

MONASTERIES

The Cistercians are an order of monks renowned for their strict austerity. During the great spread of monastic houses in the 11th and 12th centuries, the Cistercians moved into Austria. They settled on formerly unproductive land and worked very hard as agriculturalists. In time, they grew wealthy and split into two branches. One branch retained the original strict rules, while the other had fewer restrictions.

As Austria remained Roman Catholic, the Cistercians did not suffer as badly during the Protestant Reformation as did their counterparts in other countries in Europe, when Roman Catholic churches and monasteries came under attack. When the Protestant Reformation penetrated Austria in the 16th century, the monarchy and the majority of the population kept their faith.

Cistercian monasteries in Austria that were founded in the 12th century still function today, and the monks still wear the same white dark-collared cassock and black scapula. Many of the abbeys have survived by converting part of the building into a private school or by leasing out the surrounding farmland.

Statue of St. Florian. During the 4th century, Florian chose to drown himself rather than submit to the worship of the pagan Roman gods. On the site of his tomb, the Augustinian monks built a monastery that still stands today. The town around the monastery is called St. Florian.

CHOICE OF RELIGION

Austrian law on the people's choice of religious education for children is very liberal. Every young person age 14 and older can freely choose his or her religion. The state pays for religious education for every child, regardless of faith.

If the child is 10 years old or younger, the parents have the right to choose the child's religion. For children between ages 10 and 12, the parents still have the final say, although the child has to be consulted. Between ages 12 and 14, a child's religion cannot be changed against his or her will. Once a child reaches age 14, he or she is deemed to be "of full legal age" where religious matters are concerned and can choose his or her religion freely and independently.

OTHER RELIGIONS

Protestants in Austria belong mainly to the Lutheran and Reformed churches. Most live in Burgenland. In 1781 Emperor Joseph II signed the Deed of Tolerance, allowing Protestants to build chapels and appoint

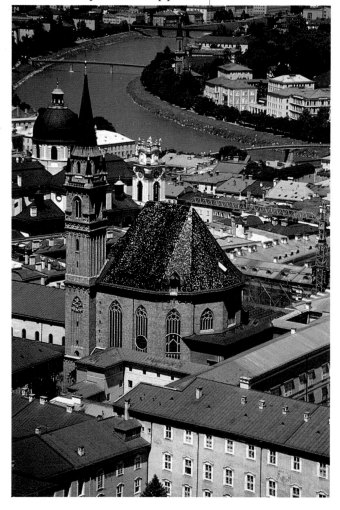

A Jesuit church. The Jesuits are a Roman Catholic order active in missionary, educational, and charitable works.

pastors. In 1861 Emperor Franz Joseph I signed the Deed of Protestants, giving Protestants the freedom to practice their faith in public. Protestants were finally entitled to equal civic rights in such areas as education and social welfare.

Vienna is more diverse in matters of religion than is any other part of Austria. Other faiths are more evident in Vienna than elsewhere in the country.

The Jews in Vienna can trace their history in Austria to the 10th century. The Jews played a vital role in the cultural life of the capital, especially at the turn of the century. After World War II, only a few hundred of the original 180,000 Jews remained in Vienna as a result of the Nazis' "final solution." Today there are about 7,000 Jews in Vienna.

Islam also has a presence in Vienna, mainly due to the influx of Muslims from Turkey and neighboring countries. In 1978 the Islamic Center was completed, providing a mosque and social services.

LANGUAGE

AUSTRIA IS THE ONLY COUNTRY—apart from Germany of course—where German is the national language. German is one of the main languages of the Western world. It is spoken by over 100 million people. There are German-speaking communities across the world from Russia to Latin America.

Austrian German does not sound the same as the German spoken in Germany. It is possible to distinguish an Austrian from a German by the way they pronounce the words.

Two general divisions of the language are High German and Low German, having their origins in the southern highlands and northern lowlands of Germany respectively. While High German is the standard written form and the medium for official communication in Germany, Austria's equivalent is High Austrian German, which is the "official" form of German used in the country.

While 98 percent of the Austrian population speak German, the minority groups have their own languages as well. Slovenian is spoken in southern Carinthia, and Croatian and Hungarian are used in Burgenland.

Below: **A wrought iron sign in German, Austria's national language.**

Opposite: **Newspaper vendors will stop by your car window on the streets of Vienna.**

AUSTRIAN GERMAN

Not only is the German spoken in Austria different from the German of Germany, but the German spoken in one part of Austria is different from that spoken in another part. The dialects in Austria are more distinct than those in Germany. A dialect speaker from Vorarlberg, for instance, could have some difficulty conversing with a local speaker from eastern Austria. In the mountainous areas of western Austria, it is often the case that the inhabitants of one valley have a separate dialect from those living in a neighboring valley only a few miles away.

A welcome sign in Styria.

The German spoken in Vorarlberg is very similar to the German used in neighboring Switzerland. This is because the people in this region have common roots in the Alemannic tribes that occupied this part of central Europe in the seventh century.

On the other hand, Vienna's dialect, Wienerisch ("VEE-ner-ish"), has developed its own unique identity. A Tirolean will recognize Wienerisch as quickly as a Californian will detect Bostonian speech. One feature of Wienerisch is the affix *erl*, which changes nouns into diminutives. For example, the word for "kiss" in High German is *kuss* ("koos"), but in Wienerisch it becomes *busserl* ("BOOS-serl").

Generally, Austrian German is softer than the German of Germany. While Germans say "KAH-fay" for coffee, Austrians say "kah-FAY." While Germans say *guten morgen* (meaning good morning) with a pronounced stress on certain syllables ("GOO-ten MOR-gen"), Austrians allow the sounds to flow more easily into one another and the sharpness is softened ("goo-ten MOR-gen").

THE LANGUAGE OF FORMALITY

In imperial times, Austrians followed strict codes of formal behavior, perhaps due to the ethnic melting pot of the Hapsburg empire and the consequent need for a common "language."

The legacy is a certain formality in the Austrian way of doing things. This is mirrored in their language. There are courteous modes of address that strike the outsider as odd, quaint, or possibly even ridiculous. A doctor, for instance, is typically referred to as *Herr Doktor* ("hare DOK-tor"), a town councilor is *Herr Hofrat* ("hare HOOF-raht"), and a lady is addressed as *gnädige Frau* ("KNEH-dik-keh FROW").

However, this formal language is merely an outward show. Underneath all the formality is a cheerful and friendly spirit. There is an often-heard saying that goes like this: "In Berlin they will tell you that the situation is serious but not desperate; in Vienna they will tell you that it is desperate but not serious."

Above: **Austrians go all the way when dressing up for a ball—just one form in which Austrian formality manifests itself.**

p89: **Signs and notices in German at the Innsbruck tourist information office.**

READING AND SPEAKING GERMAN

For a long time German was written in a Gothic style known as *Fraktur* ("FRAHK-toor"), which originated in the 14th century. *Fraktur* has been replaced by standardized Roman characters that make reading and speaking German a lot easier.

However, Roman characters are not pronounced the same way in German as they are in English. There are some rules of pronunciation that a person learning German for the first time needs to get acquainted with in order to read the letters and letter combinations correctly. Look at the few easy examples below, then try reading the words in the picture above.

LETTER(S)	SOUND	EXAMPLE
j	"y"	*ja*, which means yes, is pronounced "ya."
sch	"sh"	*Schnee*, which means snow, is pronounced "shnee."
sp	"shp"	*sprechen*, which means speak, is pronounced "shprek-ken."
st	"sht"	*Strasse*, which means street, is pronounced "shtrah-seh."
w	"v"	Raymond Weil is pronounced Raymond "Veil."
v	"f"	*vier*, which means four, is pronounced "fier."

GERMAN COMPOUNDS

An essay by the American writer Mark Twain comments on the ability of Germans to join words to form new words. This can sometimes produce extremely long words or compounds. The meaning is always very clear. As easily as they were compounded, long words can be split back into their individual components.

For example, the compound word *Volks-schullehrerseminar* ("FOLKS-SHOOL-lay-rer-SEMINAR") is made up of these words: *volks* (people or public), *schul* (school), *lehrer* (teacher), and *seminar* (seminary). Put them together and you get a "public school teachers' seminary," or in everyday English a "training college for elementary school teachers."

Sometimes the compounding can stretch anyone's linguistic ability. Try reading aloud one of the longest German words, the special title for the captain of a steamboat on the Danube River: *Donaudampfschiffahrtsgesell-schaftkapitän* ("DON-au-DAMPF-SHEEF-arts-GASAL-shaft-KAPITAN"). The words making up this compound word are: *Donau* (the Danube), *dampf* (steam), *schiff* (ship), *fahrt* (trip or journey), *gesellschaft* (company), and *kapitän* (captain).

ENGLISH AND GERMAN

Early in the Christian era, many Germanic tribes mass-migrated, some ending up in Britain where they had a decisive influence on the English language. In fact, English is a Germanic language and there are many similarities between the two vocabularies. These German words are spelled the same and mean the same in English:

blind	*finger*	*ring*
butter	*hand*	*warm*

Some of the words above begin with a capital letter. One unusual characteristic about written German is that all nouns begin with a capital letter.

Other words are so similar, although spelled and pronounced a little differently, that the link between the two languages is clear:

GERMAN	ENGLISH
Vater ("FAH-ter")	father
Mütter ("MOO-ter")	mother
Fisch ("fish")	fish
gut ("goot")	good
Buch ("book")	book
Gott ("got")	God
Freund ("FRAH-eend")	friend

More recently, the following German words have entered the English language:

kindergarten ("KEEN-DAR-gar-TEN")	kindergarten
lager ("LA-GER")	light beer
poodle ("POOD-el")	a small furry dog
hinterland ("HEEN-ter-LAAND")	the inner part of a country beyond the coast
blitzkrieg ("blitz-KREEG")	a sudden heavy attack, shortened to blitz

Even the hamburger, which seems so American, is named after the German city of Hamburg.

Street signs giving directions. In some regions, minority groups are campaigning for certain places to retain their ethnic, non-German names.

MINORITY LANGUAGES

In Burgenland, the Croatian minority are concerned about the possible decline of their language and culture, and one area of dispute has been the provision of bilingual place names.

According to the Austrian constitution, the rights of the Slovene and Croatian minorities are guaranteed. The 1976 Ethnic Groups Act provides for the rights of Croats, Hungarians, Slovenes, Romanies, and Czechs and Slovaks. However, provisions for bilingual place names still depend on whether the minority group makes up at least a quarter of the population in the area. This condition makes it difficult for minorities to preserve their culture and language, and the issue remains unresolved.

In Carinthia the minority language is Slovene. As with Burgenland's minority Croatians, the Slovenes of Carinthia, who make up 4 percent of the province's population, are fighting to keep the non-German names of their villages.

ARTS

THE 18TH CENTURY was the greatest age for Austrian music, painting, and architecture. This was partly because there were many patrons commissioning new artworks and buildings to celebrate their important status and role in society. The Hapsburgs, other noble families, and the Catholic Church became great patrons of the arts. The Hapsburgs displayed their wealth in majestic architectural projects such as the Schönbrunn Palace. The Church commissioned musicians to play for Masses and artists to decorate churches.

Below: **Artwork from the 18th century on the ceiling of the dome of the Salzburg Cathedral.**

Opposite: **A street-side musical puppet show.**

But Austria's artistic heritage does not owe everything to the aristocracy and the Church. Music has always been in the blood of Austrians. It would have been rare during the 19th century to find a middle-class Viennese family that could not put together its own string quartet.

Today, the people of Austria exhibit their artistic nature in everything they do. Their woodcarvings, glassware, wrought iron work, and embroidery show fine workmanship and an eye for detail.

VIENNA'S MUSICAL HERITAGE

Vienna has a great musical tradition. Any roll call of the world's greatest classical composers will include more musicians from Vienna than from any other city. Haydn, the Johann Strausses, Mozart, Schubert, Schönberg, and Bruckner were all Austrians. The music of Vienna had a decisive effect on the form of the symphony and the string quartet, and Vienna became the center for new symphonic writing. Beethoven settled in Vienna to work as a composer, as did Brahms. Gustav Mahler and Richard Strauss, though not Austrian by birth, are also considered a major part of the country's musical heritage.

Tree carvings in St. Wolfgang display Austrian artistic skill.

Music continues to play an important role in the lives of Austrians—from music for the folk dances of Tirol to the studied elegance of performances by the Vienna Philharmonic Orchestra and the Vienna State Opera.

Two of Austria's most important musical institutions are the Vienna Philharmonic Orchestra and the Vienna Boys' Choir. The orchestra was founded in 1842 and plays music from the classical and romantic periods. It is the world's last major orchestra to admit women; one harpist is its only female member.

The choir consists of boys between the ages of 8 and 13 and has been singing for the morning Mass in the Hofburg Chapel for 500 years. The choir often does international performances as well.

FRANZ JOSEPH HAYDN (1732–1809)

Haydn lived in Burgenland in relative comfort and ease under the patronage of two wealthy Hungarian princes. Haydn was in his time the music idol of the European intelligentsia. He made two famous trips to London and Ireland, winning great acclaim.

Haydn lived happily with the knowledge that "… I have had the good fortune to please almost everywhere…" He was interested in the structure of music and is credited with shaping the symphony into its present form.

Hadyn used folk dance music in his compositions. His *Emperor* string quartet, composed for the Austrian national anthem during the monarchy, has its musical origins in a foot-stomping dance for farmers. The dance rhythms are recognizable at the beginning and end of the piece. He also used the rustic country waltz, the *landler* ("LAHND-leh"), in his symphonies and in his oratorio, *The Creation*.

FRANZ SCHUBERT (1797–1828)

Schubert was born in Vienna and never left the city except for brief excursions in the countryside. As a member of the choir of the Imperial Court Chapel, he received the best education available

in Vienna. He was dismissed from the choir in 1813 when his voice changed. As he was too short for military service, he became a schoolteacher like his father.

Schubert composed songs, operettas, and choral pieces. He also wrote symphonies, piano sonatas, chamber music, and dance pieces for the piano. Some of his best-known music includes *The Erlking*—the tragic ride of a father trying to outdistance Death—and *The Trout*.

Schubert was a great admirer of Beethoven. When Schubert died in November 1828, he was buried close to Beethoven. The remains of the two composers were reburied side by side in 1863. The newspapers in Vienna ignored Schubert while he was alive, but printed memorial poems about him when he died. Often dismissed as only a songwriter, Schubert showed his versatility in his symphonies, sonatas, and quartets.

WOLFGANG AMADEUS MOZART (1756–91)

Mozart was born Johann Chrysostom Wolfgang Theophilus (the name Amadeus was the Latin equivalent for Theophilus) in Salzburg. His parents, Leopold and Anna Maria, had six other children, five of whom died in infancy. Only Mozart and his sister Maria Anna Walburga Ignatia survived, both musically gifted.

Mozart excelled in every musical medium of his time and is recognized as Europe's most universal composer. At age 3, he played the harpsichord and took to the violin without any formal training. He composed his first symphony at age 8 and gained fame as a child prodigy while touring Europe.

Despite an auspicious childhood and obvious talent, Mozart was not appreciated by the Archbishop of Salzburg, for whom he worked. He angered the archbishop when he declared that he, the musician, "probably had more nobility than a count." Constant quarrels eventually led to his dismissal.

Mozart traveled across Europe to find work. He was once appointed the Imperial and Royal Chamber Composer for the Hapsburg emperor Joseph II. But the grand title meant little as Mozart was underpaid and soon fell into debt.

Constant travel took a toll on Mozart's health. He died at age 35 in Salzburg, singing strains from his last work, *Requiem*. In his short life, Mozart had composed 50 symphonies, 22 operas, and innumerable other works. His music is best known for its gaiety, though it has a melancholic strain and reflects the spirit of the Enlightenment. His opera *The Marriage of Figaro* tells the tale of the struggle between a master and a servant and celebrates the dignity of the common man.

Mozart's genius was not fully appreciated in his lifetime. Legend says that he died in poverty and his wife had no money to pay for his funeral. Mozart was buried in a pauper's grave, the exact location of which remains unknown. But his music has since won acclaim all over the world.

THE WALTZ

The waltz, initially known as the *landler*, has its origin in Austria as a traditional dance in which partners come together in each other's arms, then turn with a hop and a step.

The waltz gained the interest of the upper classes, but because they were always dressed fashionably for court appearances, the waltz was gradually modified to fit their dress, which was restrictive and prevented them from moving quickly enough when they danced. Also, the ballroom floors were smooth, unlike the stone floors on which the dance was born. This too encouraged a slower waltz.

But an important element of the dance remained—close physical contact in $^3/_4$ time. As the waltz became fashionable across Europe, it provoked critics. In 1818 the *Times* newspaper of London labeled the waltz "that indecent foreign dance" and called on parents to be wary of the moral danger of "so fatal a contagion," even though partners in a waltz then did not dance as close to each other as people do in a waltz today. It was not until the end of the 19th century that people began to dance in the close embrace that now characterizes the waltz.

The most enduring and most famous pieces of waltz music were composed by Johann Strauss Sr. and his son Johann Strauss Jr. in the 19th century. Besides composing *The Blue Danube* waltz, Strauss Jr. extended the range of the waltz so that the music became orchestral in character.

Waltzers in a public ballroom. In the 19th century, such dancing was labeled indecent.

JOHANN STRAUSS SR. (1804–49) AND JOHANN STRAUSS JR. (1825–99)

Like the Hapsburg royal family that ruled an empire, Johann Strauss Sr. and his three sons —Johann Jr., Josef, and Eduard—were the kings of social dance and music who entertained at cafés in 19th-century Vienna.

Johann Sr. ran away from a book-binding apprenticeship to study the violin and music theory. In his mid-20s, he formed his own orchestra, which later became the official dance orchestra for Vienna court balls. Johann Sr. also composed more than 150 waltzes as well as music for other dance forms during his time.

Johann Jr. immortalized Vienna with his famous *The Blue Danube* waltz. When his father died, he took over the orchestra and gained even greater fame than Johann Sr. had. The younger Strauss toured as far as the United States and Russia. He also wrote operettas and other dance music. When he died, the entire "dancing Vienna" era also came to an end. A golden statue of Johann Jr. (*above*) stands in Stadtpark in Vienna.

THE VIENNA STATE OPERA

The Vienna State Opera (*below*), regarded by most Austrians as the country's cultural showcase, is a state-run institution that receives substantial subsidies every year.

In addition to the annual Opera Ball, the opera house stages about 300 performances in one season (September 1 to June 30). The Vienna Philharmonic Orchestra plays in the pit of the opera house, and the performances are possibly of the highest standard in the world.

The opera house was almost completely destroyed in World War II. It was rebuilt soon after and reopened in 1955. Today it is one of the most resplendent opera houses in the world. Yet despite its grandeur, the Vienna State Opera provides for shoestring-budget opera fans as well. Visitors can buy inexpensive standing-room tickets and stand on a graded floor with railings to lean on.

Perhaps the Vienna State Opera's greatest artistic director was Salzburg-born Herbert von Karajan (1908–89), one of the world's foremost operatic conductors. A child prodigy at the piano, Karajan studied music at the Mozarteum University in Salzburg. He turned his attention to conducting when he was 18 years old. After graduating from the Vienna Music Academy, Karajan made his conducting debut at the Vienna State Opera in 1937 and later became its artistic director.

The Austrians' love of music is best seen in the church choirs that continue to sing for the great Masses in Latin by Haydn and Mozart. In rural areas, amateur ensembles are common, especially brass ensembles playing folk music.

20TH-CENTURY MUSIC

Austria's most revolutionary composer in the 20th century was Arnold Schönberg (1874–1951). Starting out as a self-taught composer, he went on to produce the single most important innovation in post-classical music. With his *Three Piano Pieces* op. 11 of 1909, Schönberg created a new dimension of tonality, a method of composing that used 12 interrelated notes.

In the 12-tone system, the composer uses any 12 consecutive tones or notes in any order before repeating any one tone or note. Schönberg's works demonstrate an understanding of classical notions of form and technique, but abandon conventional harmony.

Another composer, Josef Matthias Hauer, evolved his own 12-tone system independently of Schönberg. Other 12-tone composers include Egon Wellesz, Ernst Krenek, Hans Erich Apostel, Hanns Jelinek, Friedrich Wildgans, and Robert Schollum.

A brass band entertains in a park.

The 20th century also saw the emergence of Franz Lehár, known as the uncrowned king of the musical comedy stage. His operetta *The Merry Widow* has been translated from German into 90 languages. Other composers of opera and orchestra music in the 20th century include Alban Berg, Anton von Webern, Erich Korngold, and Joseph Marx. Marx was a master of the more traditional, late romantic school.

Austria's rich musical heritage continues to flourish. Music is a compulsory subject in elementary and secondary schools. Fifteen- to 18-year-olds in school have two hours of music instruction each week that can only be replaced in their last two years by art studies.

A large proportion of children are enrolled in private music schools to learn an instrument, and there are advanced classes at the various private conservatories in the provincial capitals. The most advanced training is available at the three music academies in Vienna, Salzburg, and Graz. These are public institutions organized like universities, but quite independent of them. At the academies in Vienna and Salzburg, up to 50 percent of the students may be foreigners, especially Americans.

The magnificent hall of the library of the Benedictine Monastery in Admont, Styria.

ART AND ARCHITECTURE

The development of architecture in Austria owes a lot to the monks who founded monasteries and abbeys in the country and who were wealthy enough to commission large-scale projects. Early architecture in Austria exhibited the Romanesque style, following Roman models of building with massive walls to carry the weight of rounded arches and vaults.

With the rise of the Gothic style in Europe, architects began designing taller buildings, using pointed arches and stone ribs to form the vaults. Outer walls helped take the downward thrust of these high arches. Projecting from the outer walls were curved bridges connected to the arches. The bridges extended, or "flew," to the ground to take the lateral thrust of the arches, thus they were called "flying" buttresses.

This design resulted in more spacious interiors and larger windows, which in turn encouraged the use of stained glass. Gothic-style churches, with their high pointed arches that rose toward the heavens, were the product of a combination of spiritual devotion and artistic skill.

As the vaults grew higher, the artwork became more elaborate. Doorways were carved and sculptures added, first in wood and later in stone. St. Stephen's Cathedral in Vienna, which had its own workshop for sculptors, started out as a Romanesque building and was later restyled Gothic. The original building had 30,000 wooden beams supporting the roof, but this had to be rebuilt due to war damage in 1945.

Architects and sculptors were not the only artists kept busy by the Church. At a time when religion dominated so many forms of artistic expression, painters were also commissioned to add life and color to elaborately-carved altars.

In the 17th century the Gothic style of architecture gave birth to the Italian-influenced Baroque. The best of many examples in Austria of this opulent style is the abbey at Melk, originally a Benedictine abbey but rebuilt in the 18th century in the Baroque style.

The center of Vienna is an architectural treat all by itself. The ring road around the city center is the site of several important buildings, each built in a different style toward the end of the 19th century. The parliament building resembles a Greek temple, while the university has the style of an Italian Renaissance palace.

The city hall is more Gothic and Flemish in character. The most impressive of all is the Vienna State Opera, though legend has it that the building was so severely criticized when it was built that one of its architects committed suicide while the other died of a heart attack.

A mural on the entrance to a small church. The mural depicts scenes of Jesus Christ's ordeal going up Mount Calvary.

Right: **Belvedere Palace was built for Prince Eugene as a summer residence after he successfully protected the empire from Turkish invaders.**

Below: **A furnace in the Imperial Palace, Vienna, shows the opulence of Empress Maria Theresa's time.**

ARCHITECTURE FOR THE NOBILITY

Special architectural wonders include the castles and homes of the aristocrats of the Hapsburg era. A *schloss* ("shloss") is a castle or noble's residence; a *lustschloss* ("LOOST-shloss") is an aristocrat's summer or winter holiday home; and a *jagdschloss* ("YAHG-shloss") is a medieval-looking hunting lodge, with wooden beams, four-poster beds, suits of armor standing in the corners, and antlers hanging on the walls.

Many of these residences and lodges have been converted into hotels. A few, such as the Hapsburg hunting lodge at Mayerling, are now chapels. The palaces in Vienna have become famous museums, preserving within their gilded and ornate rococo walls the splendor and richness of Austria's imperial past.

LITERATURE

The most famous of Austria's early writers was Franz Grillparzer (1791–1872), who wrote long poems based on Austrian history. Some Austrian writers were not Austrian by birth but grew up under the Austrian empire that formed the language and content of their writing. One of the most significant of these was Franz Kafka (1883–1924), a Czechoslovakian by birth. In *The Trial*, he wrote about the Austrian regime as a bureaucratic police state. The poet Rainer Rilke (1875–1926) had more influence than any other writer under the Austrian empire. Rilke's poems, along with Kafka's novels and short stories, are probably the most anti-bourgeois literature associated with Austria.

Robert Musil (1880–1942) is generally regarded as Austria's greatest 20th-century writer. His most famous book, translated into English under the title *The Man Without Qualities*, dissects Austrian life on the eve of World War I. The Nazis banned the book, and Musil fled to Switzerland in 1938 with his Jewish wife. He lived there in poverty until his death, supported by friends who recognized his importance as a writer.

Stefan Zweig (1881–1942) was much influenced by the writings of Sigmund Freud. His work undermined the safe materialism of the Viennese lifestyle. An opera that he wrote the libretto for was banned by the Nazis. Zweig lived in exile in England from 1936 until he emigrated to Brazil in 1940, where he ended his life two years later, feeling that the Nazification of Europe had left him with no home.

The National Theater in Vienna, one of the many theaters where classic and contemporary dramatic works, operettas, and comic operas are performed.

LEISURE

AUSTRIANS LOVE THE OUTDOORS and take sports seriously. Skiing, the national sport and leisure activity, is so popular that a public opinion poll once suggested that a majority of Austrians ranked the current champion skier as more of a national hero than Wolfgang Amadeus Mozart. When not skiing themselves, Austrians are avid spectators of the sport, with ski races held regularly on the glaciers of the Grossglockner and the slopes around Innsbruck.

Apart from skiing, playing and watching soccer are also very popular pastimes, and the Austrian national team is usually an able contender for the World Cup. In the summer hiking is popular. With 35,000 miles (56,327 km) of mountain paths, there is room for everyone. Austria has one of the largest unspoiled landscapes in western Europe, and this has a lot to do with the people's interest in walking. There are many routes traversing valleys, hills, and snow-clad mountains. Water-skiing and sailing on Austria's many lakes are other popular sports.

Left: **An ice rink in Bad Hofgastein. Skating is one of many winter leisure activities in Austria.**

Opposite: **Hot-air ballooning in the small town of Rohrmoos, near Dachstein Mountain.**

The city of Innsbruck in Tirol has twice hosted the Winter Olympic Games.

SKIING

Austrians are introduced to skiing as early as age 3, so it is not surprising that it is their favorite sport. School trips will almost certainly include a skiing holiday at some point, either during the main season between November and April or in the off-season, at one of the year-round resorts above 11,000 feet (3,350 m). All the centers have professional instructors for all levels, from beginners to experts.

For a long time downhill skiing has been the most popular form, but now cross-country skiing, called *langlauf* ("LAHNG-lauf"), is gaining appeal. Many of the downhill slopes are getting crowded, and cross-country skiing takes one away from the crowds. It is also safer and less expensive. There are no great technical hurdles to overcome, and the beginner is spared the discouraging embarrassment of frequently falling over in the snow. The valley resorts have cross-country trails with loops and direct routes from one point to another.

A 7-year-old tries out her skis in Kirchdorf.

Austria is one of the leading skiing nations in the world. Of all the Olympic gold medals Austria has won, perhaps more than half are for skiing, and the champions who win these titles become household names. But skiing is more than just a sport in Austria; it is also an industry. Austria's ski manufacturing industry is the largest in the world, with exports accounting for the bulk of sales.

Ski tourists are attracted to Austria's ski resorts, many of which are internationally famous. Visitors find Austria's ski resorts less impersonal than many of the resorts in Switzerland and Germany and appreciate the Austrian art of *gemütlichkeit* ("geh-MOOT-likh-keit"), an attitude that creates a leisurely, warm, and friendly atmosphere full of coziness and joviality. Austrians and tourists are also drawn to the variety of activities offered in the bigger ski resorts, such as sleigh rides, tobogganing, and even yodeling.

Right: **Hiking is popular everywhere—in towns and in the mountains.**

Below: **Hot springs have made thermal baths in Bad Hofgastein a favorite leisure pursuit in winter.**

OTHER SPORTS

Austria's Alpine terrain has given rise to leisure pursuits other than skiing and mountaineering. Hang gliding and ballooning are more recent entrants on the scene. Austrians and tourists alike enjoy the thrill of parapente gliding—flying down a mountain slope in tandem with an experienced instructor by parapente, a steerable parachute. Professional Alpine climbers use the parapente as a speedy way to return home after reaching the peak.

Cycling has always been popular with vacationers in Austria, and it is common to find bicycles for rent at train stations. Specialist mountain bicycles are also available for hire, making a cycle tour of the Alps easily accessible. In the summer lakes attract water-skiers, fishing fans, and swimmers.

Apart from the more active sports, many Austrians visit health spas in various parts of the country. Some of Austria's spas are centuries old and have acquired a reputation for curing or alleviating particular medical problems.

AUSTRIAN SPORTS CHAMPIONS

Soccer star Hans Krankl helped the Austrian national team win its first World Cup in 20 years in 1978. He was voted Sportsman of the Year five times before retiring in 1989. In 2002 he became the new coach for the Austrian national team.

Niki Lauda, one of the most famous race car drivers ever, won the World Championship three times—in 1975, 1977, and 1984.

Arnold Schwarzenegger won international bodybuilding competitions before becoming a famous Hollywood action star.

The most successful Austrian skier is Annemarie Moser-Pröll. In 1971, at the age of 17, she became the youngest woman to win a World Cup for downhill skiing. Moser-Pröll went on to win another 62 World Cup victories in her career. She won silver medals at the 1972 Winter Olympics in Japan and surpassed this in the 1980 Winter Olympics at Lake Placid in the United States when she won the downhill race, the event she had always excelled in.

The only skier to come close to Moser-Pröll was Franz Klammer from Carinthia. Known as "Emperor Franz," "Austrian Astronaut," and "Klammer Express," he won five World Cup downhill titles, more than any other skier has. He reached the height of his career at the Winter Olympics at Innsbruck in 1976 when he won the downhill skiing world title.

SPANISH RIDING SCHOOL

The Spanish Riding School was founded in the 16th century to provide horses for the royal Hapsburg family. Today, the Spanish Riding School is one of Vienna's most popular attractions. The professional riders enter the school as apprentices as young as 17 years of age and spend five years learning how to train horses and at least another 10 years perfecting the art of riding. During performances, the riders wear brown uniforms with gold buttons and black hats with gold braiding.

The well-trained horses at Austria's Spanish Riding School literally dance for their audiences. They pirouette and do the capriole, that is, leap with all four legs off the ground and kick the hind legs out before landing back on the same spot.

The horses are known as Lipizzaners. This breed gets its name from Lipizza, a place near Trieste, formerly a part of the Austro-Hungarian Empire, where the stud producing these horses was located in the early 20th century. The horses are of Spanish, Arabian, and Berber ancestry. They are raised and receive their first training in the small town of Piber, Styria, before being sent to Vienna.

The famous horses of the riding school in Vienna perform in the beautiful Baroque riding hall, which was built by Fischer von Erlach in 1735. The riding hall was used as a ballroom during the Congress of Vienna (the epic conference in 1814 at which the great nations tried to reconstitute Europe after Napoleon's defeat).

Money earned from performances at the riding school is used to buy food, uniforms, and boots. The school is economically viable because the Viennese are willing to pay to watch the horses and riders perform. Today, the school turns out the most famous classical-style equestrian performers in the world.

FESTIVALS

THE FESTIVALS OF AUSTRIA are rooted in the agricultural and religious lives of the people. Agriculture and religion are related, so that Easter is not only a Christian festival based on the resurrection of Christ, but also the birth of spring and a natural time of celebration for rural communities.

Christian festivals may be celebrated with slight variations, often for practical reasons, as on the day commemorating Christ's final entry into Jerusalem to the cheers of people who strewed his path with palm branches. Since the palm is not an indigenous plant in Austria, pussy willow branches are carried in Palm Sunday processions instead.

Midsummer celebrations in Austria have a pagan origin, but the event is kept alive by rural Roman Catholics. Around June 21 each year, towns and villages all over Austria commemorate the longest day of the year with bonfires, music, and parties.

Another nonreligious festival held in early summer is the Kranzelreiten. This festival goes back to medieval days when the plague left only one marriageable girl in a village and three male survivors to contend for her hand. Today, this festival features a joust where men on horseback try to spear a ring. The reward for the winner is a *kranzel* ("KRAHNT-zel"), or wreath.

In the Fasching festival in February, parades are held in towns and villages with dancers wearing masks, hats, and fancy dress. The most famous Fasching festivals are in Tirol and the Salzkammergut region.

Below: **The Plague Memorial Column was built by Leopold I in 1679 to commemorate the end of a terrible plague.**

Opposite: **A Christmas market lights up as dusk falls over City Hall.**

115

Important festivals take place annually in Vienna, Burgenland, Carinthia, Linz, and Bregenz. The Styrian Autumn is an avant-garde arts festival designed to prompt commendation and controversy.

A crowded street in Salzburg. Located by the Salzach River near salt mines that gave the city its name, Salzburg is where thousands of people from all over the world come every year for the Salzburg Summer Festival.

THE SALZBURG FESTIVAL

Every summer Austria hosts a variety of music festivals, but the Salzburg Festival is the most famous and prestigious of them all. Max Reinhardt, the founder of the festival, was the original producer of Hofmannsthal's *Jedermann*, a version of the medieval Everyman morality play that is now a trademark of the festival. Any orchestra or opera singer invited to the festival sees such an invitation as a mark of international recognition. Salzburg was the home of Wolfgang Amadeus Mozart, so it is no surprise that his music is always the centerpiece of this annual festival.

Founded in 1920, the Salzburg Festival is now a comprehensive show with theater and opera, concerts and serenades, chamber music and live street theater, recitals and lectures. It attracts some 170,000 visitors every year, about 60 percent of whom come from abroad.

A drama performance during the Salzburg Summer Festival.

EASTER

The crucifix depicts the death of Christ for the sins of the world. Such wayside shrines are found all over the countryside.

Easter is a major Christian festival in Austria. It falls on the Sunday after the first full moon in spring and is preceded by Lent, 40 days of fasting and abstinence. As the last week of Lent ends, a service is held on Good Friday to recall Jesus Christ's death on the cross for the sins of the world. Easter Sunday celebrates the resurrection of Christ with singing, processions, and music from church bells, choirs, and village bands.

Children receive Easter eggs supposedly brought by the Easter rabbit, part of a fertility rite (both the egg and the rabbit symbolize fertility). The rabbit was the escort of the Germanic goddess Ostara who gave the name to the festival.

Less common is the ritual *schmeckostern* ("SHMECK-os-tern"), or Easter smacks. On Easter Monday and Tuesday, men and women in parts of Austria and Germany "beat" each other with birch, cherry, or vine branches in the belief that these ritual beatings bring good luck, long life, and prosperity.

CHRISTMAS

The Christmas season begins on St. Nicholas' Day, December 6, and ends on Epiphany, January 6. Cribs are displayed in homes, carols sung, and in many regions the harp provides the accompanying music.

On St. Nicholas' Day, open-air markets sell Christmas decorations and toys. The biggest celebrations are in the town of Christkindl in Styria.

On Christmas Eve, churches throughout the country are crowded with people attending midnight Mass. At St. Stephen's Cathedral in Vienna, entrance tickets have to be distributed to deal with the crowd.

Christmas Day is usually spent quietly with the family. The next day, St. Stephen's Day, is for visiting friends and relatives. On Epiphany, children go around the neighborhood singing carols and folk songs to mark the journey of the Three Kings.

Christmas decorations. The birth of Jesus Christ is celebrated throughout Austria.

The Christmas carol, Silent Night, Holy Night, *heard throughout the Christian world at Christmas time, was written by Austrian Franz Gruber. It was first performed on Christmas eve in 1818 in the village of Oberndorf. As the story goes, this carol was accompanied by guitars because mice had gnawed away at the organ's bellows.*

OTHER CHRISTIAN FESTIVALS

Corpus Christi is a religious holiday celebrated in May each year throughout Austria. It falls on the Thursday after Holy Trinity Sunday, which follows the 50th day after Easter Sunday. Colorful processions and parades take place in towns and villages across Austria, some on lakes in the Salzkammergut region. In some places Corpus Christi is an occasion to put on traditional clothes.

All Souls' Day is another event in the religious calendar when small villages come alive with a procession led by the village band, whose members wear tall white feathers in their caps. The priest often has a loudspeaker to lead the prayers and chants as the villagers walk to the village cemetery. Candles flicker by the graves that are surrounded by flowers placed there by relatives of the dead. Especially on All Souls' Day Roman Catholics pray for the faithful departed, those believed to be in purgatory because they have died with lesser sins on their souls.

St. Martin's Day is celebrated in Burgenland. St. Martin, who shared his cloak with a poor man, is the patron saint of this province and his feast day is celebrated on November 11. A special dish of roast goose, *Martinigansl* ("MAR-tee-nee-GAHN-sel"), and red cabbage is served to mark this day.

A THANKSGIVING JOURNEY

Every September 15th the Bregenzerwald village of Schwarzenberg welcomes cowherds and their cattle returning from the mountains after summer. The cowherds decorate their cattle with headdresses of flowers and ribbons and make a long journey with the herds down the Alps in thanksgiving for a safe summer in the mountains. In old times the herds were covered to protect them from demons on the journey.

FESTIVAL CALENDAR

January 1
Annual concert by the Vienna Philharmonic Orchestra; operas at the Vienna State Opera; Beethoven concerts by the Vienna Symphony Orchestra; Mozart Week in Salzburg

March/April
Easter celebrations

May 30
The Feast of Corpus Christi

May–June
A major arts festival in Vienna. Over a thousand events take place all over the city for five weeks.

June
Schubert Festival in Vorarlberg; Midsummer

July–August
Salzburg Festival; Carinthian Summer Arts Festival

September
Almabtrieb, the end of the summer grazing season when herders bring cattle down from the mountain pastures for the coming winter. The leading cow in the procession is festooned with ribbons.
Haydn Festival in Eisenstadt; International Bruckner Festival in Linz

November 11
St. Martin's Day

December 6
St. Nicholas' Day. St. Nicholas is the patron saint of children. The Christmas season begins and many *Christkindl* festivals are held.

December 24: Midnight Mass throughout the country

FOOD

AUSTRIAN CUISINE reflects the culinary influences of neighboring countries that once made up the Hapsburg empire. Austrians eat goulash from Hungary, a bean soup from Serbia, Czech bread dumplings called *knödel* ("KNOO-del"), and Italian pasta and ice cream.

The most characteristic Austrian dish is *Wiener schnitzel* ("VEE-ner SHNIT-zuhl"), a fried, breaded veal cutlet. Other kinds of *schnitzel* may use pork or turkey and may be cooked with sauce. Other typical Austrian dishes are *tafelspitz* ("TAH-fuhl-shpitz"), or boiled beef, *schweinsbraten* ("SHVINES-brah-tehn"), or roast pork, *letscho* ("LAY-choh"), or smoked bacon stew with tomatoes and red peppers, and cabbage soup.

MEALTIMES

For breakfast, Austrians have rolls and coffee, followed by *gabelfrühsttück* ("GAH-bel-FROOH-shtook"), literally a "fork breakfast," a heavier mid-morning meal resembling an American breakfast.

Lunch is the main meal of the day. It is served at noon and usually consists of soup, meat, and vegetables. Supper in the evening is lighter.

Austrians take a coffee break, or *jause* ("YOW-seh"), at around 3 P.M. to enjoy cakes and other pastries.

Below: **Austrians go to the café for an inexpensive meal and a good cup of coffee.**

Opposite: **A juice stall at Nasch Market in Weinzeile.**

A restaurant-lined street in Mondsee near Salzburg.

WHERE TO EAT

Würzelstand ("VOOR-zel-shtand"), or sausage stands, are the nearest thing in Austria to hot-dog stands in the United States. Austrians eat sausages with sauerkraut and dumplings, then wash it all down with a beer. Office workers eat at snack bars called *imbisstube* ("IM-bis-shtoo-beh") or casual restaurants called *gasthäuser* ("GAHST-HOW-seh"). Or they may decide to spend a little more at a wine cellar or wine garden—both are still less formal and costly than hotel restaurants—that serves snacks, buffet lunches, and dinners. The wine cellars started out only serving wine, but they are now visited more for the food.

Austrian dining etiquette often appears formal to outsiders. Where North Americans would comfortably use their hands when eating a sandwich, Austrians use a knife and fork. Expensive restaurants often expect their customers to wear a tie and jacket, and in Vienna even moderately priced restaurants prefer diners to wear formal dress. The general rule to outsiders is: when in doubt, dress up.

PASTRIES AND DESSERTS

The Austrians' love of food is best represented by the tempting array of pastries found in the *konditorei* ("kon-dee-toh-RAY"), or pastry shop. Pastries and desserts are collectively called *mehlspeisen* ("mehl-SCHPY-sehn") in Austria. Famous Austrian pastries and desserts include a rich chocolate cake called *sachertorte* ("SAH-kher-TOR-teh"), a sponge cake called *gugelhupf* ("KOOH-gehl-hoopf"), chocolate hazelnut pudding, pancakes called *palatschinken* ("pah-lah-SHING-kehn") stuffed with meat or a sweet filling, a sweet called *zwetschkenknödel* ("SZWETCH-ken-KNOO-del") made of damson plums (sugar lumps replace the stones and the fruit is wrapped in a dumpling), *kaiserschmarren* ("KAI-ser-SHMAH-rehn"), or emperor's omelette, and pancakes cut in pieces and mixed with jam or fruit and dusted with sugar.

A shop's tempting dessert display.

125

Many small vineyards in the Danube Valley produce new wines for local consumption.

WINE

The traditional image of dark wine cellars with countless racks of wine gathering dust as they mature over the years does not really apply to Austria. Austrian wines are characteristically light and require little maturing. This is the origin of the *heuriger*, which serves the fresh new wine of the year. Wine connoisseurs usually try a couple of glasses of the new wine and follow this with some of the older wine.

Austrian wines are not as famous as French and German wines. Each region serves its own local wines that may never reach the supermarkets. This is especially true of the wines from Burgenland. Better-known wines come from southern Tirol and Lower Austria, away from the main Alps.

Small vineyards are commonly found around Vienna and the eastern region. Toward the end of the 18th century, Emperor Joseph II's decree encouraging wine production started the development of family vineyards. Many vineyards producing wine today trace their history back to that time.

VIENNESE COFFEE

Coffee was introduced in Austria more than 400 years ago by the Turks. At that time, coffee was not yet known in Europe. Like tea to the British, coffee became an important beverage to Austrians after an enterprising Austrian merchant experimented with the brew.

Over the past four centuries, the Viennese have transformed coffee drinking into a fine art. They have created more than 20 varieties of coffee, including *mokka* ("MOK-kah"), a small cup of thick black coffee; *kleiner brauner* ("klai-ner BROW-ner"), a small cup of coffee with a dash of milk; *grosser brauner* ("groh-ser BROW-ner"), a large cup of coffee with a dash of milk; *melange* ("meh-LAHNGE"), a half-coffee, half-milk mix with a frothy crown; *kaffee mit schlag* ("kah-FAY mit shlahg"), coffee with milk and whipped cream; *doppelschlag* ("DOP-pel-shlahg"), coffee with a double portion of whipped cream; *einspänner* ("AIN-shpan-ner"), literally a "one-horse coach," actually a glass of coffee topped with whipped cream; *Türkischer* ("TOOR-kish-er"), black coffee boiled in a copper pot and served in tiny cups, and *kapuziner* ("kah-poo-ZI-ner"), a little coffee with a lot of milk.

There are many other coffee varieties, but one thing is always the same—Viennese coffee does not come without a glass of water piped in from the Alps. Some people say that this tradition is part of Austrian hospitality; others give a practical reason—to get rid of the powerful after-taste of the coffee with a sip of water.

Coffee and the news go together.

REGIONAL FOOD

A favorite hot dish in the Alpine regions, especially among skiers just in from the cold outdoors, is a bowl of *leberknödelsuppe* ("LAY-ber-KNOO-del-soop-eh"), soup with beef- or pork-liver dumplings, or a plate of *speck* ("shpeck"), smoked bacon.

A mountain resort café. Skiers warm themselves with some piping hot food.

Goulash, commonly eaten in Austria as a whole meal in itself, includes green peppers, tomatoes, onions, beef or pork, and paprika. Contrary to what many people think, goulash does not contain sour cream.

Noodles are a Carinthian specialty. They may be stuffed with cheese, meat, or fruit. Styria is well-known for its *sterz* ("stertz"), or mashes made from flour. *Türkensterz* ("TOER-kehn-stertz") is a corn mash served with soup. Another Styrian specialty is *würzelfleisch* ("VOORT-zel-fly-sh"), a pork stew with vegetables.

Fondue, a Swiss dish of melted cheese, is another favorite in Austria. White wine is heated in a casserole rubbed with garlic. Grated cheese is added, with corn-starch and a dash of nutmeg. Fondue is eaten communally, straight from the pot. Diners spear cubes of crusty bread on skewers and dip the bread into the hot cheese mixture.

SCHWARZPLENTENSCHMARREN

A popular dish of buckwheat pancakes in Tirol, *schwarzplenten-schmarren* ("SHVARTZ-plen-ten-SHMAH-rehn") is usually served with the main meal and accompanying green salads, sausages, and goulash. The Tirolean name for buckwheat is *schwarzplenten*.

Here is an easy recipe for *schwarzplentenschmarren*:

2 eggs
$1^1/_3$ pints ($^3/_4$ l) milk
Pinch of salt
Chopped chives
2 cups buckwheat flour

Beat the eggs, milk, salt, and chives together. Add the flour and mix thoroughly, making sure that there are no lumps in the batter. Pour some of the batter onto a hot pan to form a thin pancake. Fry lightly on both sides until cooked. Serve hot.

One well-known Austrian specialty is a regional dish from Burgenland called strudel *("SHTROO-duhl"). The dough is made of flour and water, and a variety of fillings are enclosed in it— apples, cottage cheese, cherries, or mincemeat.*

THE IMPORTANCE OF FOOD

In Tirol the importance of food is reflected in folktales and festivals. This may have to do with the fact that food was difficult to find during winter and survival depended entirely on the family's store of food from the summer and fall.

Winters were harsh in the mountainous regions and being prepared for the worst meant smoking or salting food and stacking firewood ready for use. Wasting food was unforgivable. The Tirolean folktale character Frau Hütt was turned into stone because she wasted food.

The importance of food is also seen in the way All Souls' Day is still sometimes observed in Tirol. All Souls' Day commemorates the souls of the dead and the belief that souls not yet purified for heaven may be helped by prayer. In parts of Tirol and northern Italy, this is linked to a belief that the dead may return on All Souls' Day. So strong is the belief that food is left overnight on the kitchen table for returning souls.

GOULASH

This recipe serves four people.

5 pounds (2.3 kg) beef shank or shoulder	6 cups water or chicken stock
4 tablespoons oil	2 bay leaves
2 pounds (0.9 kg) sliced onions	3 tablespoons dried marjoram
1 tablespoon sugar	1 tablespoon finely chopped thyme
3 tablespoons tomato paste	1 tablespoon finely ground caraway seeds
8 tablespoons paprika	8 cloves of finely chopped garlic
5 tablespoons vinegar	Salt and pepper

Cut beef into large cubes. Add oil, onions, and sugar in heated Dutch oven. Sauté until golden brown. Add tomato paste and paprika. Deglaze immediately with vinegar and water or chicken stock. Bring mixture to a boil, then add beef cubes, bay leaves, marjoram, thyme, caraway seeds, garlic, and salt and pepper. Cover and simmer for $1^1/_2$ hours or until meat is tender. Serve with potatoes (boiled in water spiced with a pinch of caraway seeds). Alternatively, goulash may be eaten with Austrian bread dumplings.

SACHERTORTE

1 cup butter
6 ounces (170 g) unsweetened baking chocolate
1 cup confectioner's sugar
8 egg yolks
1 cup flour
Vanilla

10 egg whites
4 tablespoons apricot jam
1 cup sugar
1 cup water
7 ounces (198 g) baking chocolate

Cream butter. Melt 6 ounces chocolate in a double boiler. Add gradually to creamed butter the melted chocolate, confectioner's sugar, and egg yolks, one by one, stirring constantly. Add flour and a dash of vanilla and beat well. Beat egg whites until stiff and fold into batter. Pour mixture into a well-greased 10-inch (25.4-cm) round mold. Bake at 300°F (149°C) for about an hour. Let cool and turn out of mold. Cut cake in half, horizontally. Spread heated and slightly diluted apricot jam over lower half of the cake. Replace top, brush with apricot jam, and cover with chocolate frosting. To make the frosting, boil sugar and water until sugar is completely dissolved. Melt 7 ounces chocolate separately in a double boiler. Add sugar syrup gradually to chocolate, stirring constantly. When cooled, frost the cake.

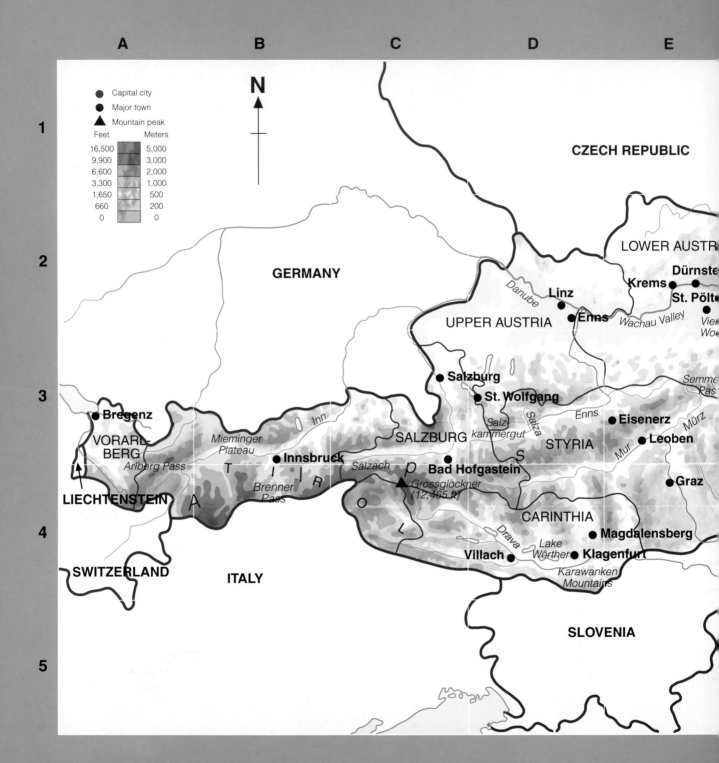

A B C D E

1

N

Capital city
Major town
Mountain peak

Feet		Meters
16,500		5,000
9,900		3,000
6,600		2,000
3,300		1,000
1,650		500
660		200
0		0

CZECH REPUBLIC

LOWER AUSTRI

2

GERMANY

Danube

Linz

Krems

Dürnste

St. Pölte

UPPER AUSTRIA

● **Enns**

Wachau Valley

Vie
Wo

Salzburg

St. Wolfgang

Semme
Pas

3

● **Bregenz**

**VORARL-
BERG**

Inn

Mieminger
Plateau

SALZBURG

Salz
kammergut

Salza

Enns

Eisenerz

Mürz

Arlberg Pass

A

T

I

R

Salzach

S

STYRIA

Mur

● **Leoben**

LIECHTENSTEIN

Brenner
Pass

O

Bad Hofgastein

▲ Grossglockner
(12,465 ft)

● **Graz**

CARINTHIA

4

SWITZERLAND

L

Drava

Magdalensberg

Lake
Wörther

● **Klagenfurt**

ITALY

Villach

Karawanken
Mountains

SLOVENIA

5

F

SLOVAKIA

VIENNA

Leitha

Hainburg
Forest

● Eisenstadt

*Lake
Neusiedler*

RGENLAND

HUNGARY

CROATIA

MAP OF AUSTRIA

Alps, A4, B4, C3, C4, D3
Arlberg Pass, A3, A4

Bad Hofgastein, C3
Bregenz, A3
Brenner Pass, B4
Burgenland, F2–F4

Carinthia, C4–E4
Croatia, D5, E5, F4, F5
Czech Republic, C1, D1, D2, E1, E2, F1, F2

Danube (river), A2, B2, C1, C2, D2, E2, F2, F3
Drava (river), C4–F4, F5
Dürnstein, E2

Eisenerz, E3
Eisenstadt, F3
Enns, D2
Enns (river), D2–D3

Germany, B2, B3, C1–C3
Graz, E4
Grossglockner, C4

Hainburg Forest, F3
Hungary, F3–F5

Inn (river), A4, B3, C3
Innsbruck, B3

Italy, A4, A5, B4, B5, C4, C5, D4, D5

Karawanken Mountains, D4, E4
Klagenfurt, D4

Leitha (river), F2–F3
Leoben, E3
Liechtenstein, A3, A4
Linz, D2
Lower Austria, E2, F2

Magdalensberg, D4
Mieminger Plateau, B3
Mur (river), D4, E3
Mürz (river), E3

Lake Neusiedler, F3
Lake Wörther, D4

Salzkammergut, D3
Salza (river), D3

Salzach (river), C3
Salzburg, C3, C4, D3, D4
Semmering Pass, E3
Slovakia, F2, F3
Slovenia, D4, D5, E4, E5, F4
St. Pölten, E2
Styria, D3, D4, E3, E4, F3, F4
Switzerland, A3–A5

Tirol, A3, A4, B3, B4, C3, C4

Upper Austria, C2, C3, D2, D3, E2

Vienna, F2
Vienna Woods, E2, E3
Villach, D4
Vorarlberg, A3, A4

Wachau Valley, E2

ECONOMIC AUSTRIA

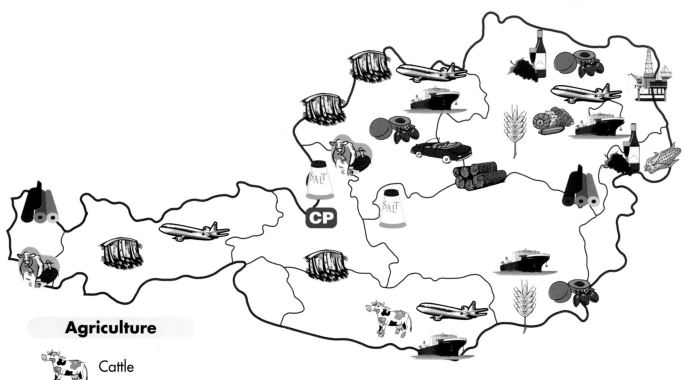

Agriculture

 Cattle

 Corn

 Dairy Products

 Fruit

 Vegetables

 Wheat

 Wine

Natural Resources

 Copper

 Hydroelectricity

 Oil

 Salt

 Timber

Manufacturing

 Textiles

 Vehicles

Services

 Airport

 Port

ABOUT THE ECONOMY

GDP
US$203 billion (2000)

GDP SECTORS
Agriculture 2.2 percent, industry 30.4 percent, services 67.4 percent

LAND AREA
32,367 square miles (83,830 square km)

LAND USE
Arable land 17 percent, cultivated land 1 percent, pastures 23 percent, forests and woodland 39 percent, other 20 percent

AGRICULTURAL PRODUCTS
Grain, potatoes, sugar beets, wine, fruit, dairy products, cattle, poultry, lumber

INDUSTRIAL PRODUCTS
Machinery, vehicles, food products, wood, paper, chemicals

CURRENCY
The euro (EUR) replaced the Austrian schilling (ATS) in 2002 at a fixed rate of 13.7603 Austrian schillings per euro.
1 euro = 100 cents
USD 1 = EUR 1.03 (August 2002)
Notes: 5, 10, 20, 50, 100, 200, 500 euros
Coins: 1, 2, 5, 10, 20, 50 cents; 1, 2 euros

LABOR FORCE
3.7 million (1999)

UNEMPLOYMENT RATE
5.4 percent (2000)

INFLATION RATE
2 percent (2000)

MAJOR TRADE PARTNERS
Germany, Italy, Switzerland, France, the United States, Hungary

MAJOR EXPORTS
Machinery and equipment, iron and steel, paper, textiles, chemicals, food products

MAJOR IMPORTS
Machinery and equipment, metal goods, oil and oil products, chemicals, food products

PORTS AND HARBORS
Enns, Krems, Linz, Vienna

AIRPORTS
55 total; 24 with paved runways (2000)

TOURIST ARRIVALS
17.8 million (2000)

INTERNATIONAL PARTICIPATION
European Union (EU), Food and Agricultural Organization (FAO), Organization of Economic Cooperation and Development (OECD), United Nations (UN), World Health Organization (WHO)

CULTURAL AUSTRIA

Skiers' paradise
Serious skiers are particularly attracted to St. Anton in the Arlberg for its challenging courses. Slopes fall in all compass directions, and the longest run stretches 5 miles (8 km) from Valluga to St. Anton. The resort also offers friendly courses for families and older skiers. The crowds usually come late November through Easter.

Eisriesenwelt ice caves
First discovered in 1879, this system of underground caverns near Werfen is characterized by frozen waterfalls and other ice formations. Visitors can join a 75-minute lamp-lit guided tour through the world's largest ice caves between May and October.

Hohensalzburg Castle
Europe's largest fortification stands 94 feet (120 m) above the city of Salzburg. The castle served as a residence for archbishops during the 15th and 16th centuries. Today artists come here from around the world to attend courses held by the International Summer Academy of Fine Arts.

Stone Age discovery
In 1908 the Venus of Willendorf, a 4.4-inch (11.2-cm) limestone statuette, was discovered near the town of Willendorf in the Wachau. Believed to be around 26,000 years old, this icon of prehistoric art now sits in the Naturhistorisches Museum in Vienna.

Hofburg Palace
Built between the 13th and 20th centuries, the palace was the residence of the Habsburg monarchy until 1918. Today it is the seat of the presidency and a state-of-the-art international convention center. It also houses historical and cultural collections and the National Library.

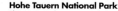

Hofkirche monastery
This Franciscan monastery in Innsbruck houses the tomb of Emperor Maximilian I (1458–1519), where there are 28 bronze statues representing his ancestors and marble reliefs showing scenes from his life. Next to the Hofkirche is the Tyrolean Regional Heritage Museum.

Hohe Tauern National Park
This protected area spreads into the Carinthia, Salzburg, and Tyrol provinces. Here stands Austria's highest mountain, the Grossglockner. The country's first national park was established in 1981 and gained international status in 2001.

Graz old town
The capital of Styria was declared a UNESCO World Heritage Site in 1999. Visitors can take a tram up the 1,552-foot (473-m) Schlossberg hill. Here stands Graz's landmark clock tower, which unlike other clocks tells the hour by its long hand and the minutes by its short hand.

Semmering Railway
Built in the mid-1800s, the Semmering Railway has been named a UNESCO World Heritage Site in recognition of the quality of its tunnels and viaducts, which are still in use today. Passengers can board the train at Vienna and enjoy a scenic mountain ride to Graz.

Haydn Music Festival
During this internationally renowned annual festival in September, classical music lovers get to enjoy Josef Haydn's music in a historic environment. Many landmarks in Burgenland's capital are linked to Haydn, such as the house where he lived, now a museum.

ABOUT THE CULTURE

OFFICIAL NAME
Republic of Austria

NATIONAL FLAG
Three horizontal strips, white in the middle sandwiched by red at the top and bottom

NATIONAL ANTHEM
Österreichische Bundeshymne. Opens with "*Land der Berge, Land am Strome*" ("Land of mountains, land on the river"). Text by Paula von Preradovic, melody from a masonic cantata by Mozart.

CAPITAL
Vienna

OTHER MAJOR CITIES
Graz, Innsbruck, Linz, Salzburg

POPULATION
8,150,835 (2001 est.)

ETHNIC GROUPS
German 98 percent; Croatian, Czech, Hungarian, Slovak, Slovene, and other 2 percent

RELIGIOUS GROUPS
Roman Catholic 83 percent; Protestant, Muslim, and other 17 percent

MIGRATION RATE
2.45 migrants per 1,000 population (2001 est.)

OFFICIAL LANGUAGE
German

LITERACY RATE
98 percent

INTERNET USERS
2.6 million (2000)

TIME
Greenwich Mean Time plus 1 hour (GMT+0100)

IMPORTANT ANNIVERSARIES
National Day (October 26), May Day (May 1)

LEADERS IN POLITICS
Kurt Waldheim—Secretary-General of the United Nations, former president of Austria (1986–92)
Thomas Klestil—president since 1992
Wolfgang Schuessel—chancellor since 2000 and leader of the People's Party

FAMOUS MUSICIANS
Anton Bruckner, Franz Joseph Haydn, Herbert von Karajan, Wolfgang Amadeus Mozart, Arnold Schönberg, Franz Schubert, and Johann Strauss Sr. and Johann Strauss Jr.

OTHER FAMOUS AUSTRIANS
Sigmund Freud (psychologist), Oskar Kokoschka (painter), Andreas Nikolaus Lauda (car racer), Robert Musil (writer), Arnold Schwarzenegger (movie star), Ludwig Wittgenstein (philosopher)

TIME LINE

IN AUSTRIA	IN THE WORLD

10,000 B.C.
End of Ice Age in central Europe

753 B.C.
Rome is founded.

450 B.C.
Celtic tribes enter Austria.

116–17 B.C.
The Roman Empire reaches its greatest
extent, under Emperor Trajan (98–17).

30 B.C.
The Roman Empire expands into Austria.

A.D. 400s
Romans withdraw. Germanic tribes
and Slavs occupy Austria.

A.D. 600
Height of Mayan civilization

A.D. 788
Austria becomes part of
Charlemagne's empire.

A.D. 955
Austria becomes an independent state.

1000
The Chinese perfect gunpowder
and begin to use it in warfare.

1278
Hapsburg dynasty begins.

1530
Beginning of trans-Atlantic slave trade
organized by the Portuguese in Africa

1558–1603
Reign of Elizabeth I of England

1618
Habsburgs rule Austria and
a large part of Europe.

1620
Pilgrim Fathers sail the *Mayflower* to America.

1683
Ottoman Turks attempt unsuccessfully
to capture Vienna.

1776
U.S. Declaration of Independence

1789–99
French Revolution

1861
U.S. Civil War begins.

1869
The Suez Canal is opened.

IN AUSTRIA	IN THE WORLD
	1914 World War I begins.
1918 Austria fights in World War I. Hapsburg dynasty ends. Austria becomes an independent republic.	
1938 Nazi Germany invades Austria.	
1939 Austria fights as part of Germany in World War II.	**1939** World War II begins.
1945 Allied forces (United States, Britain, France, Soviet Union) occupy Austria.	**1945** The United States drops atomic bombs on Hiroshima and Nagasaki.
1955 Allied forces withdraw; Austria becomes independent.	**1949** North Atlantic Treaty Organization (NATO) is formed.
	1957 Russians launch Sputnik.
	1966–69 Chinese Cultural Revolution
1985 Jörg Haider, leader of the right-wing Freedom Party, wins 10 percent of the vote.	
1986 Controversy over war record of elected president Kurt Waldheim	**1986** Nuclear power disaster at Chernobyl in Ukraine
1989 Hungary begins dismantling its border with Austria.	**1991** Break-up of the Soviet Union
1994–95 Freedom Party wins 22 percent of the vote. Austria joins the European Union.	**1997** Hong Kong is returned to China.
2000 Freedom Party joins coalition government; other European Union nations protest.	**2001** World population surpasses 6 billion.

GLOSSARY

anschluss ("AHN-shloos")
Union of Austria with Germany after the 1938 German invasion.

dirndl ("DURN-duhl")
Traditional dress for women consisting of an embroidered blouse, a lace bodice, a full skirt, and an apron.

föhn ("foehn")
A warm, dry wind that blows from the south across the mountains in spring and autumn.

gemütlichkeit ("geh-MOOT-likh-keit")
A jovial attitude that establishes a warm and friendly atmosphere.

heuriger ("HI-ree-geh")
A wine tavern that serves fresh, new wine produced each year.

High German
A division of the German language that originated in the German highlands. High Austrian German is the "official" form in Austria.

jause ("YOW-seh")
A mid-afternoon coffee break.

konditorei ("kon-dee-toh-RAY")
A pastry shop where customers can sit down to have coffee and pastries or order to take out.

langlauf ("LAHNG-lauf")
Cross-country skiing.

lederhosen ("LAY-der-HOH-sern")
Traditional dress for men consisting of leather shorts with ornamental suspenders and a belt.

Lipizzaner
A breed of horse developed for the Hapsburg emperors and used today at the Spanish Riding School.

Österreich ("OOST-er-rike")
The name for Austria meaning Eastern Kingdom.

sachertorte ("SAH-kher-TOR-teh")
A famous Viennese cake filled with apricot jam and iced with chocolate.

schloss ("schloss")
A castle or residence of nobility built during the Habsburg era. Many have been converted into hotels.

strudel ("SHTROO-duhl")
A light pastry with various fillings.

social partnership
An arrangement where management and trade unions meet to negotiate wages and prices.

waltz
A three-step dance, characterized by formal slow steps or whirling fast steps.

wiener schnitzel ("VEE-ner SHNIT-zuhl")
A fried, breaded veal cutlet.

FURTHER READING

BOOKS

Ake, Ann. *Austria*. California: Lucent Books, 2000.

Beer, Gretel. *Austrian Cooking*. London: Andre Deutsch, 2001.

Brook, Stephen and Deni Bown. *Eyewitness Travel Guides: Vienna*. New York: Dorling Kindersley, 2001.

Cooper, Barry. *Master Musicians: Beethoven*. New York: Oxford University Press, 2001.

Pick, Hella. *Guilty Victim: Austria from the Holocaust to Haider*. New York: I.B. Tauris, 2000.

Roraff, Susan and Julie Krejci. *Culture Shock! Austria*. Oregon: Graphic Arts Center Publishing Company, 2001.

Vergo, Peter. *Art in Vienna 1898–1918*. London: Phaidon Press, 1993.

Wolfgang Amadeus Mozart and Robert Spaethling (translator). *Mozart's Letters, Mozart's Life*. New York: W.W. Norton & Company, 2000.

WEBSITES

Austrian National Tourist Office. www.austria-tourism.at/index_e.html

Austrian Parliament. www.parlament.gv.at

Austrian Press and Information Service in Washington, D.C. www.austria.org

Central Intelligence Agency World Factbook (select Austria from the country list). www.cia.gov/cia/publications/factbook

European Parliament. www.europarl.eu.int

Federal President of the Republic of Austria. www.hofburg.at/index_ie.html

Lonely Planet World Guide: Destination Austria. www.lonelyplanet.com/destinations/europe/austria

Republic of Austria. www.austria.gv.at/e

The World Bank Group (type "Austria" in the search box). www.worldbank.org

World Travel Guide: Austria. www.wtg-online.com/data/aut/aut.asp

MUSIC

Angelic Voices: Best of the Vienna Boys' Choir. Polygram Records, 1999.

Beethoven and His Pupils. Koch International Classics, 2001.

Strauss: The Best of Vienna. Polygram Records, 1999.

VIDEOS

Austria: Innsbruck. Education 2000 Travel Series, 1994.

Austria: Summer in Austria. Education 2000 Travel Series, 1994.

Austria: Vienna and the Danube, Salzburg and the Lakes District. Questar Inc., 1998.

BIBLIOGRAPHY

Bousfield, Jonathan and Rob Humphreys. *The Rough Guide to Austria*. London: Rough Guides, 2001.
Brook-Shepherd, Gordon. *The Austrians: A Thousand-Year Odyssey*. New York: Carroll & Graf, 1998.
Greene, Carol. *Austria*. Chicago: Children's Press, 1992.
Hadley, Leila. *Fielding's Europe With Children*. New York: William Morrow, 1984.
Hamilton, Freddy. *Insight Guide Austria*. London: APA Publications, 1998.
Hewett, Jonathan (editor). *European Environmental Almanac*. London: Earthscan, 1995.
Lye, Keith. *Take a Trip to Austria*. New York: Franklin Watts, 1987.
Lye, Keith (editor). *Today's World: Europe*. New York: Gloucester Press, 1987.
Matthews III, William H. *The Story of Glaciers and the Ice Age*. New York: Harvey House, 1974.
Ventura, Piero. *Great Composers*. New York: G.P. Putnam's Sons, 1989.
Austria in Pictures. Visual Geography Series. Minneapolis: Lerner, 1998.

INDEX